Praise for *Approaching the End of Life*

"Rev. Schaper has produced a book that is thoughtful and helpful for those who will open themselves to considering the part that death and dying play in living and life. Written mostly from a Christian perspective, it nevertheless has insights and refreshing, light, and honest views on approaching these issues that are applicable to all persons in every faith, and none." —**Rabbi Joe Blair, administrative dean, Gamliel Institute of Kavod v'Nichum; coordinator, Jewish Values Online; Bridgewater College**

"Reading this book made me excited to live and die well! I am in my thirties and, technically, not approaching the end of life. However, Donna Schaper's perspective on ending life at a place of peace and composure makes the hard topic of death totally comfortable, accessible—and inspiring! I am already planning the best funeral ever and living life to the fullest so that when that funeral happens, it can truly be a celebration for all in attendance!" —**Carissa Reiniger, founder and CEO, Silver Lining, Ltd.**

"While Schaper says this book is about 'dying,' it is just as much about living. The reader is encouraged to embrace death (and life!) with 'spiritual honesty' in the context of a postmodern, pluralistic twenty-first century. Her words have caused me to take pause and reflect upon how I am choosing to live each day in preparation for a wonder-full end, instead of an inevitable conclusion. I am filled with a profound sense of hope. I want all the people I love to read this book." —**David R. Gaewski, conference minister, New York United Church of Christ**

"With fresh language and a helpful breadth of perspective, Rev. Donna Schaper has provided an invaluable tool for approaching the end of life, a must-read for clergy and highly accessible for laity. I will be looking forward to using *Approaching the End of Life* as a solid text on practical spirituality with adults in my parish." —**Ron Bretz**

"Regarding the aspect of death, I have to look at it from many angles, from my practice, their families, my family, and myself. In any scenario, it can be difficult on how to react, what to say, and how to feel. Rev. Schaper does an excellent job of discussing a potentially difficult or challenging matter in an upfront, logical, and very caring way. I think everyone needs to read this book." —**Scott Jurica, MS, DC, PAK, ACN; holistic doctor**

"Approaching the end of life, complex emotion and mundane decisions collide. Grief mixes with mystery. Donna Schaper is a wise, experienced guide through the colliding, the grief, the mystery, and the intimacy of that tender time. She writes with the power of long experience and careful observation, sharing stories of approaching death well by living well. She writes with deep appreciation for people in and out of faith communities, giving all of us generous ways to honor the momentousness of dying. And she writes convincingly that the best moment to begin preparing for our inevitable end is right now, with close attention to the troubles and grace that make up both a good life and a holy death." —**The Rev. Dr. John A. Nelson, pastor and teacher, Niantic Community Church, CT**

"Donna Schaper's new book is the ideal vehicle for tackling an urgently essential teaching for our times. Who should read it? Pastors, old and new, who need new tools to help those knocking at their door without the culture of a congregation. Individuals who have managed to avoid the topic of mortality until an embarrassingly mature age who now must create something for themselves or a loved one. And even those of us professionals who have failed in our own lives to begin important processes like retirement planning or life review. She shows us that preparation for death can be a fulfilling and often joyful exercise of discovering value in our unique and communal identity. Read it." —**Rev. Carrie Bail, interim pastor, First Congregational Church of East Longmeadow, MA**

"This is a book for those who wish to embrace the end of life with open arms. May all our inevitable passings be filled with such powerful ministry!" —**Caroline Woolard, cofounder, OurGoods.org and TradeSchool.coop**

"In our death-defying culture, how welcome to have this new book that teaches us not only how to have a good death and playfully imagine the great mystery beyond, but also how to live the fullest life. Part Garrison Keillor, part Anne Lamott, Schaper leans into a decades-long ministry to share with us stories and deep truths that will make readers laugh and cry and think and feel their way to healing and wholeness." —**The Rev. Dr. Katharine R. Henderson, president, Auburn Theological Seminary**

"Donna Schaper writes about how we respond to death—our own and others—in ways that are both wise and practical. In so doing, she helps us engage the most important realities we will ever face and equips us to talk about them with those we love." —**Martin B. Copenhaver, president, Andover Newton Theological School**

"Donna Schaper looks squarely at the rich fullness of life without flinching—even when life's last event inevitably arrives. This candid assessment of death and its leading days is an exercise of the deepest core values, she says. This courageous book, with its lively and intelligent tone, ingeniously loops back to how we live our lives now. What a freedom in that." —**Rev. George E. Packard, retired bishop of the Episcopal Church**

APPROACHING THE END OF LIFE

A Practical and Spiritual Guide

Donna Schaper

ROWMAN & LITTLEFIELD
Lanham • Boulder • New York • London

Published by Rowman & Littlefield Publishers, Inc.
A wholly owned subsidiary of
The Rowman & Littlefield Publishing Group, Inc.
4501 Forbes Boulevard, Suite 200, Lanham, Maryland 20706
www.rowman.com

Unit A, Whitacre Mews, 26-34 Stannary Street, London SE11 4AB

British Library Cataloguing in Publication Information Available

Library of Congress Cataloging-in-Publication Data

The hardback edition of this book was previously cataloged by the Library of
Congress as follows:

Schaper, Donna.
Approaching the end of life : a practical and spiritual guide / Donna Schaper.
pages cm
Includes index.
ISBN 978-1-4422-3824-4 (cloth : alk. paper) — ISBN 978-1-4422-3825-1
(electronic) — ISBN 978-0-8108-9562-1 (paperback)
1. Funeral service—Planning. 2. Terminally ill—Religious life. 3. Death—
Religious aspects. 4. Spiritual life. I. Title.
BV199.F8S36 2015
248.8'6175—dc23
2015008612

Printed in the United States of America

"When you pass through the waters, I will be with you;
and through the rivers, they shall not overwhelm you."
—Isaiah 43:1

CONTENTS

INTRODUCTION

Approaching the End of Life is a practical and spiritual guide to dying well and if not well, optimally, and if not either well or optimally, then conscious that you have prepared yourself excellently for one of those options. Who do I mean by "yourself"? I mean you as you try to prepare for your own death. I mean those who want to be prepared for the death of a loved one. And I also mean those who are just putting their toes into the water of the giant subjects of death and dying. It is written as though someone has come to my office at the church where I am a minister and wants to know how to do a funeral or memorial for a loved one. The tone is matter- of-fact and frank. It is also gentle and conversational.

I will know that my client(s) have lived a lot of years before this visit—when plans could have been made or weren't made—and that they may have a lot of years ahead of them. I will wonder how to get enough trust together in a short period of time to do something that actually takes a lifetime and a folk culture, intertwined, to accomplish. The point is not just a good funeral but also a good death, which means a good life. I will wish I had prepared the broken communal infrastructure around death and dying with the same hope that Con Ed has about the broken gas line or the

Metropolitan Transit Authority has about that broken switch—the hope that the break could have been prevented, but now the break has happened. I am writing this book to repair what is broken.

Are we any different today in our dying than we were in years or generations past? Yes, we are. We don't have a homogeneous culture that tells us what to do. In this book I am not interested in reestablishing a homogeneous culture but instead offering multiple paths to a good death that embrace our diversities. We can either say we have lost our folk culture or that we are on our way to a new kind of culture. Jews would call my writing a kind of *tikkun olam*, the repair and restoration of the breach. At least after the book is written, I will have fewer regrets about what I and we could have done earlier. Pete Seeger says my intention well in his song "Quite Early One Morning." He urges us to heed early warnings.

What I mean by "end" in the title is actually a double entendre. It is about time and its purpose and the purpose in time. As a good friend of mine says, she lives by the rule of three: "What?" "So what?" "And now what?" These three rules will take you straight to the point of time. What is the point of time? It is having a good time in time. "Good" is also filled with double meaning: we are to have a fun time and a virtuous time. By end I mean the objective of life, realized, by the end time of this life. If you realize your own objective, purpose, or point in life, early enough and often enough, you will come to have the "best funeral ever." That was the title I wanted for the book but the editors thought it too competitive. It is actually not competitive at all, just a way of saying that dying well is living a custom-designed life. The best funeral ever is the best one for you and no one else. Likewise the best life is the one for you and no one else.

We changed the title to *Approaching the End of Life: A Practical and Spiritual Guide* to soften the blow of knowing that it is now quite early in the morning. We have time to prepare and the time is now.

As Elizabeth Gilbert, author of *Eat, Pray, Love,* says in one of her TED Talks, "The point of life is to find something you love more than you love yourself and head straight towards adoring it." You can have the best funeral ever by being the best you ever. You can approach the end of life practically and spiritually by finding something you love and aiming at it, every day, while you are alive, so that regret is eased at the end. You can achieve your person long before you die, and in that living, take away death's sting. The worst funeral ever comes straight out of not finding your point or purpose or way early enough to live into it. The worst funeral ever comes from not aiming toward goodness.

As will become clear, I believe we live on as spirits and die "only" as historical and biological beings. I am writing this book about approaching our ends from the point of view of the multiverse, not the universe. I believe, with most scientists today, that we are one universe among many, one bubble among many bubbles, on our way to the ninth or tenth sky. "Ashes to ashes, stardust to stardust" is a phrase you will hear over and over throughout this book. That cosmic grandness does nothing to diminish but instead enhances the importance of our living and our dying. We are part of the great awesome. We are blips in the great awesome. It would not be itself without us and our genome. We are becoming not dust but stardust, scientifically and spiritually.

This guide is not just for my parishioners—I know them and in general know what "folk culture" they want to use. They are part of our congregation because they trust it to help in the big transitions. This guide is also for the ones I don't know—who outnumber the ones I do know. This guide aims to repair the breach of a broken folk culture which is also an opening folk culture. We are learning new ways to ritualize the ends of our lives, just as we are learning new ways to work, communicate, marry, and raise children. One kind of folk culture is being replaced by another. When we proactively take care of our living and our dying, we create a new folk culture, more appropriate to the social economy that has already come among us.

Many people still come to a parish or priest or imam or rabbi at the time of death. They want to "take care of it" in an hour—and what I know is that it takes a lifetime of intention to have the best funeral.

In a way, we are always writing our own obituaries, day by day. We are also planning for that final edit, when in that remembering hour or so our lives are completed and reviewed. The best funeral ever happens when it is always being readied. We are prepared for the end long before we actually end. We are fully prepared for death when it can no longer surprise us or the folk who will surround us as we part and pass.

This book also answers the question of what we want for our memorial or funeral by giving examples of best practices and real choices that people have made. It will help you prepare for the inevitable while driving you more deeply into your ordinary days.

My mother-in-law got the news of a lump in her breast and went on the most frantic housecleaning I have ever seen. Every drawer was completely tidied, every closet reordered, all corners of the attic swept. Why? "Because I didn't want to leave a mess behind for someone else to clean up." Ah. The breast lump proved benign. And she had a very well-organized house. This book is about arriving at your biological end with a house in good order—and hoping that you get to enjoy knowing that completion for a good long time. Benign is not the right word for that enjoyment; the word is peace. It is also composure. This is a guide first to peace and composure and then to dying well—which together allow the best funeral ever to happen.

Because I myself am a postdenominational Christian, married to a Jew for thirty-two years, raising three adult children in both

Christian and Jewish observance, I have had a rich education in postdenominational rituals and living. I don't think of this mixture of mine as something that is broken so much as I think of it as something evolving. I do know that many are evolving into new practices with me. At our funerals or memorials, there will be a great mixture of people, most of whom are open to many ways of ritualizing our endings. Some will vigorously not believe in God, others will have their rosaries in their hands. I have also been an ordained Christian pastor in the United Church of Christ for forty years and have officiated at hundreds of funeral and memorial services. My congregations have filled up with people who used to call themselves Nones, many of whom call themselves atheists or agnostics. Yes, I have had an odd perch. I have had a front-row seat on the end of one kind of religion and the beginnings of another.

This guide is for people who don't know (yet) how to have the best funeral ever. It will take them into the land of reality about how real people do real funerals and memorial services—and will give them permission to enter the competition for a personal "best" for themselves and those they love. Remember, I said optimal or well or at least not surprised by death. Personal best encompasses the optimal, the well, and the active persistent refusal to be surprised.

Denominational and postdenominational people of all faiths and traditions will be interested in this twenty-first-century, welcoming theology that gives practical and honest help about how to die and how to ritualize dying. Those who choose to prepare themselves for their ends will find this guide to infrastructure repair useful. Those who "don't even want to think about it" might also want to read further as a way to dip their toes into the experience of their own passage. It will be particularly useful to Nones and people who have moved around a lot and are without a folk tradition for the end of life. A book can't be a folk tradition or repair a broken one. It can be a guide to how to repair a broken folk tradition and how to build one for yourself.

For example, people use the words "funeral" and "memorial service" interchangeably. Tradition-based people know that a memorial is a service without a body; a funeral is a service with a body. Very few people today, even within religious traditions, understand that distinction. Likewise, many think that a eulogy is a funeral sermon. It is not. A sermon at a funeral or memorial is for the living and about God and the meaning of life and is directed at those who will die next, not at the deceased. A eulogy eulogizes the deceased and puts the focus on him or her. When a funeral or memorial has only a eulogy, it makes the world as small as the individual. When it also has a sermon, it enlarges the world. When I yearn for postdenominational, plural, twenty-first-century folk traditions and point a way to them, I am also yearning for a large world where we help each other make meanings and don't leave that great task up to the individual or nuclear family alone.

I am not judging the confusion so much as trying to reach for it with an appreciation for honest spirituality and religion, both not either. My concern is for people who are stranded by their own and their institutions' confusion about basic matters. We live in a multiverse, not a universe. We will also die in a multiverse. Getting ready for that death is important, if for no other reason than that it removes the matter from your unconscious and subconscious and wakes you up to one of the most interesting of all facts of life. You will die. I will die. This book says, "Get over it and get into it." It addresses life's greatest adventure, dying, and argues that at least during this adventure we should be stretched enough to give our core values a little exercise. Indeed we are but wayfarers here, but what a way it is.

THE END OF LIFE TODAY

Edie Clark tells a story about how funerals are changing, even in stodgy New England. She reported a couple who blew their ashes out of a cannon over the town lake, and a woman who had an enormous collection of perfumes, which her heirs put out for the congregation to try on before the funeral. Those allergic had to leave. An auctioneer painted the church building white so it would look great for his funeral—and then had a rehearsal at his auction house where he wanted to hear what everybody had to say. Brass bands and New Orleans jazz are coming into their own at funerals, as is a more joyful note. People don't like morbid anymore. Even in the most traditional of parishes, many voices join the eulogizing and more and more frequently, there is an open mike.

I'm not going to answer the question of why things are changing so much as to tell you that they are. The dam has burst on the right way to do a funeral. Multiple options exist and are socially accepted. Some people even choose not to have a service at the end. Why? They don't see the point nor are there many social or religious or cultural police who would insist that they do. A great tolerance pervades: if that is what they want, then let them do it. That tolerance has virtues and it also can veer into individualism. You surely want your own individual meaning expressed at the end of life. And you also want to have a sense of community and connection.

If I do have a criticism about the multiple ways we do rituals at the end of life today, it is here. When I went to seminary, forty years ago, we were taught to speak of the big meanings of death in our funeral sermons. Today, people mostly just want eulogies, which are custom designed for the life that has been lived. Eulogies are a search for meaning at the end. They sum up. We have gone from universal meanings about death, grounded in faith traditions, to speaking of the value of the individual. I love speaking of the value of the individual and mourn the loss of more general meanings about death. When I do a funeral or a memorial, I try to include both a general sermon, to comfort those left behind with meaning, and words that honor the individual. I conclude with a translation of the old commitment sentence "ashes to ashes, dust to dust," which says instead "ashes to ashes, stardust to stardust," because I want to give the survivors a sense of meaning about death. Call my translation a postmodern reach for a scientifically based religion or call my translation a way to be inclusive of many traditions. Call it green and embracing of the grand spirituality of evolution. Whatever you call it, know this: it is what people remember about the funeral. They leave comforted around their own death and not just comforted around the loss of the individual they have eulogized.

Folk ways of dying are being replaced with modern and postmodern ways of dying, if for no other reason than we are early in multipath and "none of the above" ways of living. Theologian Diana Eck says we are moving from diversity to pluralism, a place where difference is normal. This book is for the plural, those who don't know how they should die because they imagine so many ways being acceptable. As we move to populations, as Eck says, with more than 50 percent being Nones, we will find the pressure to create meaningful moments at death increasing. Even the Nones will want something more beautiful than tolerance. They will want tolerance plus meaning. They will want eulogies and sermons, and if not sermons, then at least some comfort for themselves.

Medicine also contributes its part in the big change: we die differently, 70 percent in hospitals, even though 70 percent say they want to die at home. Because the way we die *is* changing, so are the ways we let our dearly departed depart. Here I offer some critique of the medicalization of death, but not as a jab or a complaint. There is more to death and dying than being hooked up to a machine that beeps a lot. There are enormous assets in the way we die today and many of us are still alive because of those beeping machines. There are also deficits. It is important not to let medicine take up too much space and to open the space for religious and spiritual meaning at the end.

Hospice also has made the death experience both easier and more accompanied. It is also true that in hospice we hire the help we need at the end, as opposed to caring for our own in our own ways. This is not a negative judgment of hospice! Hospice does what many families no longer can do, without losing their jobs or their homes to landlords who won't like wheelchairs in the elevator. There is no need to romanticize the past. Instead, there is a need to realize that extended families took care of their own. Today extended families don't live close by and a job can be lost in weeks of attention to an ailing or dying relative. A few decades ago people were "laid out" in their own living rooms and bathed and dressed by their survivors for that moment. That practice is actually coming back in the "environmental burial movement." So is its opposite, an increasingly antiseptic approach, where the funeral director handles everything, even the service in the funeral "parlor." More than one person I know has divided their ashes between favorite places, some at sea, some in the Rockies, some in the backyard. We are rapidly adopting new patterns for dying. Again, we can appreciate what the funeral director does for us and with us—at a cost—and we can open up the space for more than just one way to be cremated and distributed.

My sneaking suspicion about why funerals have "lightened up" and become memorial services where the body is banished has to do with the word "challenge." You hear it all the time. People soften up human suffering with language that makes it sound manageable. Death becomes just another "challenge" when clearly it is much more than that. Here I try to be soft about human suffering because I know it is not manageable. Even the quietest and most peaceful death, in one's sleep, at home, leaves a huge void in those left behind. I write to open up the space for suffering and for solace and to keep the "details" of dying in their proper places.

Not all deaths are peaceful nor are all excruciating. Some deaths are excruciating, others are not. Many are part peaceful and part excruciating. More and more people sign papers giving their relatives permission to let them go if the pain becomes too much near the end. We are changing into funeral "lite" because our capacity to bear the heavy is so far gone. "Challenge" is just a weak word for dying. Dying is so much more than a challenge. Whatever problems you have with religion or tribalism or uniform cultures, at least they told us what to do when we died. Eck's forecast of pluralism may be wonderful, as I believe it is, but it can also throw your daily living and dying into a tizzy. Become spiritual but not religious, marry a Jew or a Christian, become a multiracial couple and watch the folk culture go out with the vows. In this introductory chapter I frame the deficits of postmodern, postcultural people and bring them into assets. Pluralism is good, very good, and even godly. The chapters that follow build on the deficits and show us how to live in our time, without nostalgia, and with a sense of spiritual assets. Tolerance is necessary but not complete as a virtue or value. Developing rituals within pluralism is a joyful task, one that death and dying invites us to enjoy and engage. This book teaches rituals at the time of death and excites a muscle called action and reflection as a way to become able for walking the bridge to new traditions and new communities. Action-reflection is nothing more than a habit of thinking about what you do before and as and after you do it. That way you are free to not do everything the undertaker or clergy person advises, while also respecting tradition, expertise, and community.

Here I give practical and spiritual guidance on how to bear the heavy, if it comes our way, and how to bear the light, if it comes our way. I give practical and spiritual guidance about living in pluralism, which I more than enjoy and appreciate. I am not sure there is a great difference between the practical and the spiritual. One informs the other to go back and reinform the other. The practical and the spiritual spiral together into rituals of meaning. My point is about readiness, to be ready for death and strong for it, despite the loss of a folk culture or a "way we do things." Instead of cultural or religious police, instead of worrying about the right way to die and ritualize death, here I open the multi-path, multiverse conversation. We do need rituals and rites and will back into them or head toward them. Here I recommend heading toward them instead of backing into them. I recommend spiritual proactivity instead of spiritual reactivity.

The big division in the world is not between the sacred and the profane or the practical and the spiritual. It is between the sacred and the desacralized. When we pay insufficient attention to the practical and spiritual aspects of dying, we desacralize death and die unready. We die with less meaning than is possible attending us and those we love. We become as small as our decades or ourselves and turn our back on the great gifts of human community and connectedness. We turn both life and death into inconsequentiality. Neither is inconsequential. Both are consequential. The service you choose and the preparation you make for your end resacralizes what is desacralized. It also gets you beyond the eulogy into the meaning making. You don't need a priest or pastor to make the meaning or give the sermon. You may want to make meaning out of individual value. That is the trick and asset of a good ritual.

Only one service is right as a rite for you and yours. Likewise, there are many good ways that you could die. Why not prepare for the best one? Or the optimal one? Or the ones most deeply conscious and connected? Why not aim for stardust with your full and most personal genome intact?

I

THE BEST FUNERAL EVER

In this chapter, I tell you about some funerals and memorial services. Some of the names are disguised but the people are real. Others have given permission to tell their story. I only tell some of the parts of each because all of the parts would overwhelm you.

First, there is the call from the family or the funeral director. Someone has died. The undertaker or funeral director has been called by the hospital to pick up the body. There is the immediate follow-up with the family or chief mourners. There is often telling somebody who doesn't know, like a distant relative or a divorced spouse. Then there is the negotiation of the meeting to plan the service or the observance. Once I met with a bereft son whose mother had jumped off a building to her death at 1 a.m. We met at 4:30 a.m. that morning. Then there is the service itself and the planning and the event machinery put in motion. Then there is the follow-up. But for now hear about some very different services.

None of them is for you. I offer them in hopes that they will encourage you to think in a custom-designed way about yourself and the day your show closes, bringing the curtain down for the last time. I do not offer these services for you to imitate them, although borrowing a trick or two is always a good idea.

H. M. "HARRY" KOUTOUKAS[1]

Harry was as unlikely a person to have a Greek Orthodox Eucharist for his funeral as they come. He was a cigarette-smoking former serious drinker and drugger who loved nothing more than a
good AA meeting. He liked nudity in the many plays he wrote and
he made irreverence a steady virtue. "Suck" appears to be one of
his favorite words. To say that Harry was a homosexual is to
understate the obvious. He called me "The Rev. Dr. Cupcake"
and had a passion for giving everybody a nickname, some more
sweet than others. The week of his death he asked me to come
over and give him communion. That was the first serious signal
that he knew the time had come. His twin brother was high up in
the Greek Orthodox Church and had been forbidden for years to
even talk to Harry. When the twin died last year, Harry began to
go. He loved his brother, in the same way he had of loving life. He
knew how mean it was but found a way to not notice. Wit was his
way.

His voicemail said, "Leave a message, especially if you can say
something interesting." Needless to say, that message was intimi-
dating. Very few of us have the wit of Harry. Some people never
miss an opportunity to miss an opportunity. Harry was the opposite. He never missed a chance to quip or quarrel or change your
point of view on what had just happened. In his corrections, he
often had a way of shoveling your sentimentality into a cuter
bucket. His closer friends love to say that he had the freedom to
relax from his opportunistic quipping. "I love being here at
brunch with you where I can just be and not also be entertaining."
He had a way of keeping you simultaneously intimidated and

---

1. This account was previously published in the *Villager* newspaper, March
17–23, 2010, with full permission from his family, only one of whom is left
alive.

amused, inspired and appreciated, sometimes with a quip that could bite your toes off.

Speaking of toes, Harry was a diabetic. His trick was that of the clown who often shows us how happy we could be about how sad we are. Harry said, "I can't even get a discount on a pedicure, even though I only have eight toes." His fans ranged from the famous to the fallen, from Yoko Ono, who was his neighbor when first he came to New York and continued as his patron, to the three kids from the pier who created the shrine for Harry that adorned Christopher Street in the days after he died. The kids reported that it was Harry who understood them, even though their parents had thrown them out and the cops were chasing them. What could they do? They put candles and flowers on the altar of his "Glittermobile."

Which leads to the Glittermobile. Judson Memorial's (our church) relationship to Harry was as parish to parishioner. He was one of those people who showed up with vigor in the offering plate and in the pew, which is a movable chair at Judson. Toward the end our relationship to Harry was primarily through his Glittermobile. When Harry could no longer navigate standing up, we asked Yoko Ono to buy him a vehicle. She did. Judson owns the vehicle but Harry had lifetime use. Harry nicknamed it the Glittermobile. He let its battery run down so many successive times that we had to insist that he not by refusing to get it recharged. The lack of attention to the Glittermobile's needs (not to mention that he had to park it next door to his fifth floor walk-up apartment at the neighboring church, where they should have but did not charge him for charging it) resulted in fairly nonstop groans at the Judson office, where one staff member after another said "I am not doing it, whatever it is." After a couple of years, the company from which we bought the Glittermobile went out of business. That means that only bribery gets us new parts. The Glittermobile (sort of) continues to function and is looking for a new home as we speak. I am considering the Smithsonian. Its latest role as shrine is going to make it very picky about its new place.

A purple-haired, fur-coated, bird-on-shoulder man will no longer cross the meeting room on Sunday mornings to go out for a smoke during my sermons. I will miss these "interruptions" while knowing that they were frequently the full message. It is rare we get such good examples of shortcoming in the middle of a service. "Smokers for Jesus" was a real organization at Judson; Harry was its president. Judson is not very big on the short and instead worships the "loving God" whom Harry knew. Harry's driving the Glittermobile in front or behind the table always told us more about the loving God than the cigarette. His theology was that of love and he had more ammunition for the punishmentalists than anyone I know. I so wish Glenn Beck could have debated him. Wit was the ammunition. H. M. Koutoukas won an Obie in 1965 for "Assaulting Established Tradition." His behavior in worship did the same but never with scorn. That was another of Harry's tricks: he could intimidate you by being so smart, so witty, so "on," but then he would make sure he sent you a Valentine's Day postcard and sign it "Love, Harry." Harry had little of the scorn the world had for him.

As he often said, "You can pretend to be serious but you can't pretend to be witty." He also had a joy that must have been difficult with emphysema. The quote most people want to give you about Harry—now that we are deep in his quoting season—is, "If you see a child go by, be sure to tell them how beautiful they are." One of those "children," Sarah Kornfeld, has posted a remarkable piece from her history of growing up at Judson. Check out www.WhatSarahSees. Her take on Harry is antistyle and prosubstance. She argues that Harry was fundamentally smart and that his style often distracted from our seeing his brilliance. She says he was the "full integration of style and substance." We were so overwhelmed by the wit and the style that we couldn't quite get to the ideas. I agree with this child of Judson and want to take her comment one step further. Harry only looked antireligious. Religion or faith or spirituality, pick your clunky word, was at the heart of this Greek Orthodox man. It is not an accident that he wanted a full Greek Eucharist at his final service. I couldn't get him to do a living will, or assign a surrogate, or make any end of life plans. He joked me along whenever I mentioned them. One day though he called up to ask for the full Greek Eucharist, which we did with vigor and solemnity.

Religion was so much against Harry but he was not against it. His big ideas were love, joy, irony, paradox, sentimentality's hook pushed all the way through your skin to the other side. My favorite song of his, which we also sang as part of the "full" Greek Eucharist, remains "The Rhinestone Crucifix."

Harry was often described as self-destructive or at best self-limiting. He would announce plays that never happened, refer people who wanted to publish or produce his work professionally to a possibly nonexistent Swiss agent, and became the subject of several legends about fantastic brawls and shenanigans, one involving him throwing a famed Off-Off producer down a flight of stairs. He encouraged such stories. His response to my pushing him about his archive and his will was to say that several men in shiny suits were going to show up saying they owned the archive and that I was to throw them down a flight of stairs. He also constantly said, "Don't give it to New York University, even over my dead body."

As Off-Off Broadway expanded, he said he was going to make a fortune with a bus that would take tourists from the 7 o'clock show at the Cino to the 8 o'clock at La Mama, the 9 o'clock at Judson Poet's Theater, and then the 10 o'clock at Theatre Genesis. If you don't believe me about the love thing, and its penetrating ironies and the paradox of Harry being its protégé, just take a look around at how many were on the bus for his two funerals.

Yes, two. We had to move in chairs for his first service, which happened impromptu on the night he died, giving yet more meaning to the movable feast that Harry was. A couple hundred people just showed up.

One of the dozens of speakers at Harry's first service said, "Beware of nostalgia." I think Harry would agree. The bus will make different stops in this new century. Harry won't be on it. But his loving style and loving substance will be.

At his second service, the Glittermobile, his name for his best friend, was placed at the front of the service, wearing its customary Christmas lights. After that we pushed it, empty, past all his favorite haunts, and at each one the parade picked up, ending at his apartment. By the time we got to his apartment, there were several hundred people marching. Harry would have liked the parade. The message on his phone answering machine had said, "If you don't have something interesting to say, please hang up." Harry was not a candidate for a traditional or stationary memorial service. A single man, Harry's service attracted more than four hundred mourners. They needed a way to say good-bye to Harry even more than Harry needed to say good-bye to them. And yes, we had the full Greek Eucharist, even though his father, the bishop, and his twin brother were not in attendance. Harry had the best funeral ever, for him and those who love him. Not loved him, but love him. That love goes nowhere. It becomes part of the great stardust when our body's ashes are gone.

J AND D

You might also have liked J and his son, D, who died within a year of each other, one from anger, and the other from AIDS. The father had not forgiven the son for being gay. And the son had not forgiven the father for murdering his own father, after discovering him making love to a farmworker at their Long Island Duck

Farm. J was not always the man he hoped to be, nor was D the man he had hoped to be. Both had lives that were damaged by tragedy. D got AIDS before there was a cure and died at age twenty-nine. J spent seven years in jail and returned to his family and business and church to be a well-respected usher. Neither died with their lives complete. Both memorial services could not survive the truth of the minor key in them. People wept "extra" because there was no way around the unfinished part of either life. Almost exactly the same people came to both services, which was about two hundred. The actual services were very similar: the Navy hymn ("Eternal Father Strong to Save," ending with a plea for those in peril on the sea), joined by Psalm 139, each man's favorite. There was a strong reach for the power and forgiveness of Almighty God for a father and son so publicly estranged. And there was also finally the power of praise for life, even when it is not perfect or complete. You might think that people would want to stay away from the suffering of this father and son and their wife and mother but just the opposite happened. People wanted a way to come close.

J was fully forgiven by his community and his congregation, but he did not attend his own son's funeral. At J's funeral, a year later, the sting remained. J who had been forgiven could not forgive. He also ruined his son's funeral for his beloved wife, who stuck by his side the seven years he was in prison. Funerals are no place for hate. When somebody important doesn't show up, their absence sucks all the air out of the room. You don't have to be perfect to have the best funeral ever. Instead you have to be connected to communities, which have a strong tendency to forget what you could not.

C

C was a cleaning woman at a local college. She was the poorest person in our church and also its most steady contributor. She lived alone, even though she came from a family with nine children. C was the first but not the last person to tell me about the incest she knew from her father. She lived in senior housing sponsored by the town. She put five dollars in an envelope each week to give to the church, even though it meant she only took part of her pills instead of all to make "her tithe." Because she took care of my infant for the first year of his life, sitting with him in one of the pews while I worked at the church office, I became very close to her in her retirement. I gave her a diamond ring that my first husband had given me for our engagement. It seemed like the right thing to do for a woman who never married and deserved something beautiful. C had become part of our family. When she died, I found notes in her will that said, "Give the diamond ring back to Donna when I die so she can make somebody else happy with it." She also wanted to sing "My Lord What a Morning" at her service. That's all we knew. Those were her last wishes. We sang the heaven out of "My Lord What a Morning." C had dozens of people, not hundreds, at her funeral. She learned how to make friends late in life and never did forgive her father. She did forget him and move on, moving on so much that she knew how to love somebody she would never know. C's intelligent disposition of the ring made such good sense. I often advise people that their jewelry is very important to their having the best funeral ever.

M

Often the funerals and memorials we remember the most are the happiest and most serene ones. The hard ones disappear into that place where we have learned how to protect ourselves from the pain that breaks through our defenses. Let me resurrect one very painful one that ended with two Ninja Turtles going into a grave alongside a seven-year-old boy in one of those small caskets that we never want to see. There is no reason for M's parents to read this book. They had no chance to get ready. M's mother had an accident with M, age seven, in the car. Both "walked away," only to discover that M's very slight spleen had split in the impact. He died six hours later. What I knew as a pastor was that it wasn't the first or second day of impact for the mother, the father, and the older sister but the lifelong change that would matter. The mother now twenty years later, on the anniversary of M's death, sent me a note. "I still can't forgive myself. Why did I dare to imagine he was OK?" The father now twenty years later, on the anniversary of M's death, still doesn't talk much about it, despite the whole family being in and out of therapy for years. He says, "I can't." He says he will explode if he does and he has to try not to explode so he can go to his telephone pole fixing job for the day so he can support the family he has left. The older sister—who became an only child within six hours—lost her own childhood, was compelled to take care of her mother, began to resent M, whom she only knew for seven years, and still feels the burden of being a grown-up because one minivan hit another when she was only nine. She is now a successful journalist with a dark streak right across the middle of her own spleen. Death marks us, every time. We go into the funeral as one person and come out as another.

This book is not for people who have no chance to prepare for death. It is for people who do have a chance to prepare. I may be writing this book because I was hit by a drunk driver, a year later by an eight-point buck, after my tenth anniversary of surviving breast cancer. In each case I escaped death and was forced to realize that it wasn't just my parishioners who were going to die. Mortality had its plans for me too. When death becomes real as opposed to something fuzzy and foreign, we think about what we might do while alive to make its arrival as good as possible.

SHERMAN

Sherman died from an infection after a simple knee operation. He was only fifty-eight. His wife put together a state-of-the-art slideshow with his favorite music, summarizing all three parts of his life: his youth, his first marriage and its offspring, who were present at the service, with their offspring, and then his life with her. His first wife was also present but not in charge. Susan was clearly the chief mourner and she took her responsibilities seriously. She did it with a deftness that included everyone and slighted no part of Sherman's life. She found a way to include rather than exclude, with technology and photographs at her side. She had pictures of his prom next to pictures from their last cruise together. She paid equal attention to each of the three grandchildren, giving a gift to children forever. "Here I am on Grandpa's lap." Everyone who came to the service was given a copy of the slideshow. Susan starred at the service, as the new matriarch of the new family. That was not her intention, and that is why she starred.

Susan chose to have the memorial service three months after Sherman's death. She wanted to do this extraordinary summary of a life and to present it well. Her choice was widely respected and appreciated. Often in a life that has many different parts the best funeral ever comes out of observation of the different parts, not in ignoring them. The act of observation brings them together and brings a coherence to what others might mistakenly see as chaotic.

JANE

Jane was a 4-H county executive who planned her service so much that it even included a rehearsal. She died of a long, slow, and serious cancer that allowed her to be fairly well until the final rounds of chemo. She picked out the clothes she would wear when "laid out," down to the earrings and the stockings. She picked out the scriptures (23rd Psalm) and the hymns ("Amazing Grace" and "Blest Be the Tie That Binds"). She chose the menu and preordered it from the caterer. She also paid the undertaker and all the bills and placed a generous honorarium for me in an envelope written in her hand. Spencer, her husband, a wealthy contractor who could not bear the loss of the woman for whom he lived, was sidelined. Did it bother him? No, he said, this was just the way he wanted things. Jane had managed every one of their house renovations, she managed all their trips, and she managed their affairs. Why should she stop managing now? The service she created was for herself and for him. The life they lived informed the death she had. For the dress rehearsal, Spencer brought three dozen yellow roses, extravagantly arranged. She loved the surprise. Indeed this book is about being ready for death and its rituals. You might want to overdo it like Jane did, and then again you might not. Knowing why you would overdo or underdo—or hit a balance in between—will tell you a lot of what you think about the point of time and the point of life. The best part of preparing for the end is the clarification of your own values on the way.

MARY

Mary died at age forty from breast cancer, leaving her daughter and husband bereft. They just couldn't deal with the unfairness of it. The daughter had one kind of inconsolable grief, the husband another. She had a most traditional service at the church, open casket, three hymns, two scriptures, one eulogy, prayers, and then a powerful graveside service. She was very clear, as was her husband, that she believed in the resurrection of the body and life after death. She was almost the opposite of Roz, who comes next, as she clung to the Christian Easter theologies. She was not scared of death at all, but she was terrified at what would happen to her husband and her daughter. She was right to worry. At the graveside, the husband and daughter both grabbed the coffin before it went down, "ashes to ashes and dust to dust," as if neither knew that the other was going to break down at all. They each all but tried to go into the grave with the casket. Instead of consoling each other, they stared silently and greedily at their own loss. Finally, the funeral taker and I intervened, each taking one back to the car. I went back later that day to the graveside because I felt very incomplete about Mary, owing to the dramatic events with the coffin. There I found Gary, her husband. He was weeping. Her grave was very close to their house, as the cemetery was right behind their neighborhood. He went there every day for two plus years, no matter the weather. He just couldn't let her go. Finally, I saw him after I was no longer pastor in this church. "Gary, do you still go to Mary's grave?" "No, one day I just decided not to go. And that was the day I knew she was really gone, and that I would be OK." Mary's daughter now has two children. Life does go on. But sometimes people have the best funeral ever by dragging it out for two years.

Who are any of us to judge people who love each other so much that they can't imagine getting along without them? And if that question pierces, think of it as a good one about becoming both dependent on another and independent of them. Mary's anticipatory grief about her own death was incomplete: she could only worry about "others" and there was little room for self. We owe it to each other to become fully ourselves as well as fully connected. Again, the clarification of our values as wayfarers on the road to a certain end is valuable. It may or may not decrease the grief or the suffering of those left behind. But it also is the only thing that can.

ROZ

Roz died at ninety-six, after begging people to let her go, informing everyone she was more than ready. She had a wonderful life, she was ready to go, and life did not interest her any more. Her son, sixty-five, was not as happy at her interest in departure as she was, but there was no quieting Roz. She often wandered around town on late summer nights, buttonholing people she might meet, telling them she wanted "to go." Roz insisted there be no prayers or mention of God at her service, lest it make her agnosticism look hypocritical. She didn't even want a service but wiser voices prevailed and said, "At least have a potluck and let people speak." The potluck was a feast, the words were powerful and funny, the son was comforted, and Roz had her way. Preparing for your end may be a minimalist decision: you may want to mean it when you say "I want something very simple."

ANITA

Anita was a hard person to bury. She was so opinionated that it was hard to get her right. You couldn't get her opinions out of the way. I gave the eulogy, by invitation of my best friend, who is Anita's daughter. She had her service in a Catholic Church where she "won" her argument that there should be no hymns and no casket. The priest welcomed my Protestant voice—and you could tell he was amused at Mrs. Houston's final commands, having been a veteran of them his whole life. The eulogy I gave for her is appended here, showing one pattern for giving a eulogy. I like three parts sweet, one part sour, or three parts positive, and one part negative, just to show that we know what people are really like. When I do a sermon, I often try to use parts of the eulogies as examples for what I want to say. I want to assure us that none of us are perfect at the same time that I assure us that God's love is perfect and comes to all of us equally. At times of death and its separations, the most important thing to speak to is God's powerful grace. It is large enough to hold the pain. Plus, I dislike the sentimentality that tries to make people too sweet. It is harmful to the human spirit and doesn't help mourning at all. Mourning will find its way to the sweet and the sour. An eighty-six-year-old woman told me with a twinkle in her eye and grace in her heart that she was mad at her husband, of equal age, for getting cancer. She was real. She was gracious toward herself. She knew she was missing a mark and that she was not being her best self. And she also wanted to be truthful instead of fictional. If truth is good at the end, and also throughout life, why not help it along?

Eulogy for Anita Houston, March 22, 2007

I used to call her Mrs. Houston, and then she became Anita. You can understand how strange that move was for me. This was a woman who knew how to tell the local police that she would keep on driving, despite their concerns. She told the priest no hymns and today her will has prevailed. I am so glad we are having this service on her beloved husband Ike's birthday: it is right that this simultaneity occur.

A eulogy has a short job description. It is to commemorate the person, assess his or her life, and to give solace to those often left behind. I often use another triplet to structure eulogies. Three virtues and one vice. You will see both organizational tools at work here.

Mrs. Houston managed to liberate herself from the cage of the private. There is an old and bad joke about how the true place of the clergy is in the stands with the women and children while the real men play the real game on the real field. Mrs. Houston wanted to play on the real field, and she did. The UN has been the beneficiary of this decision, as have many, many international families. Her enemies were mediocrity (as anyone who didn't get into Yale knows), indignity, bunk, flummery, domesticity, sentimentality, privatization, and bad manners (as anyone who ever forgot to send a thank you letter knows). She fought the revenge life takes on distinction. She was "interested in everything and nothing less," as Murray Kempton put it so well, long ago. On her deathbed she wanted the *New York Times* and not poetry read to her. The field, not the stands, was her destination in life. Need I say how unusual this was in a woman?

Secondly, she knew that she mattered. She took upon herself the "obligation to be wonderful," as Mary McCrory said of Nance McDonald in her eulogy for her. She had an impetuous honesty, an articulate eloquence, and an agile fury. She was less nice than noted. If Anita was in the room, everyone knew it.

She also had the virtue of civic connection. Her friends were the old-fashioned virtues of civility, decorum, will, character. If you dared, you could call her a do-gooder. The telephone was her technology. She was a spider, if we need an animal for her. She had the virtue of web, net, connection. When you got a phone call from Anita, you knew you had been phoned.

Again, on her deathbed, she was true to character. Anita died after wowing us at her deathbed with what at first glance was a virtue. She was intubated, could not speak, but could write. She wanted desperately to tell us something; you could tell by what was left of her body and its language. We gave her a pad. On it she scrawled "water." We thought she was thirsty. We told her she was fully hydrated, just not by mouth. We thought we had comforted her. We were wrong. She returned to her vigorous "no" head turning. We tried again. She scrawled, "Water . . . the plants." Anita was one-third samurai, one-third Eleanor Roosevelt, and one-third Mother Superior. Even at the end she was telling us what to do and for whom and what to care. You could call it a virtue. I call it a vice. On our deathbeds, those of us who think the point of life is to care for others, which it is, might learn to receive care. In fact, the people who can't receive often can't really give. We often oppress the poor by not equalizing the giving and receiving in charity. Or better yet, grace is that time when we can't tell who the giver is and who the receiver is, so blended in joy are they. Anita may not have fully achieved that joy.

Like many a man, whom she oddly resembles more than most women, vulnerability came to her late in life. She was easier to admire than to love. Warm and fuzzy, no. Warm and prickly, yes.

As we ourselves pause at the gate, we find solace in these facts. She had ninety-four good years. She lived them "her way." We can predict a family diaspora: Anita was a weight-bearing beam. [The family diaspora did happen and actually quite quickly, when no longer commanded.]

Anita knew it was time to turn her lamp off. Her dawn has come. We can almost hear her saying right now, the "speaker has gone on too long."

By the way, the plants will be fine.

CONCLUSION

You were not Harry or Anita. You were you. That is the best funeral ever. I would call each of these services "the best funeral ever," because they had spiritual honesty to them. By spiritual honesty, I mean a fit to the person and their lived life. They also qualify for the personal best because they helped the people left behind. Spiritual honesty can be just someone singing Sinatra, "I

Did It My Way," at the service, and leaving everybody else cold. Well, the beloveds might say, what about me? The best funeral ever suits the person who has died and helps those they leave behind. Help is defined as comfort, existential and personal, and also a sense of completion. We enter the service as one person, we leave as another. That entrance and exit are the true marks of a ritual: we are changed by what happens in the sacred space. We will never be the same again. Our community and our traditions have told us we are going to be OK, even though all is now changed.

A funeral or a memorial has one more purpose, beyond fit and comfort. It has a great chance to use words and music and scripture to help the living understand the point of life. In the eulogies, we tell each other what matters. In the hymns and the scriptures we relink to God or what little we can know of God. We "just have to be there" or "just have to be together at a time like this," because otherwise our despair will get the best of us. What despair? The kind that most people have most of the time and that all people have some of the time. Old-time pastors don't even like eulogies, so convinced are they that the death rituals are the best time to bring people to their knees. By knees, I mean the place where we are struck at our core and remember that we have one. When services go too "lite," we miss the great opportunity to do battle with our despair on behalf of our core purpose. Each of the services I describe above filled this third purpose as well as the first two. They did comfort. They did sum up the life of the deceased. And they also told the gathered what was important about life and how we can face, together, the sorrow we will surely see.

Some of these services were traditional, which works for some people, and some, like the recent Yankees innovations, almost tell tradition to get lost. In each case the bereaved had the chance to plan something that was suitable. Sue took a good long time to get

Sherman's service together. She wanted to grieve by going through things—and the family was far flung enough that they could wait to schedule a memorial that would accommodate school and airline schedules. Most people want a memorial much quicker so they can get "over it" and "on with it." Again, the best funeral ever is what accommodates the mourners as comfort and the dead person as spiritually honest. Death is no time to lie.

If we are lucky, we will have time to mark our end with spiritual preparation and honesty. If we are not, like Matthew and his family, death will have much more of a victory over us than it merits. The reader should take special note of what happened to Matthew and his family. Prepare.

If we take the time to improve our luck by trusting and tutoring our aim toward the best funeral ever, we ourselves will die accompanied by peace and we will leave peace and an increased sense of purpose to those who remain. There is nothing small about that peace.

2

WHAT TO DO WHEN YOU GET SICK AND DEATH FIRST KNOCKS ON YOUR DOOR

When we are sick, we often use that (sick) joke: "I wish I were dead." In fact being sick is a good rehearsal for being dead. We slow down, we often lie down, and we ache in mind or body. Most people die lying down. Most people ache on the way out. Some ache a long time, others go quickly. Certainly there is slowness to death, which is remarkable. When dying, we rarely rush off to another place. In fact, many people report that observing a death involves a sense of time having stopped.

If you think being prepared for death is a quick or simple matter, you are wrong. Preparing for death is like the reconciliation part of the truth and reconciliation commission, made famous in South Africa by Bishop Desmond Tutu. You will recall that the South African bishop led his country through a process of forgiveness known as "truth and reconciliation." He often said that many people could manage the truth that they had been hurt or hurt another. But very few had the muscle for the reconciliation process. Reconciliation is a long journey. It can take months, even years, and even when you think you are complete or finished, something can happen to tell you that you are not. You can imagine you have forgiven the man who murdered your mother only to have a nightmare that you have taken up a sword against him. Likewise the preparation for death: the truth is easy. We don't know anyone who hasn't died or won't die. But reconciling ourselves to this truth is much harder. In fact, most of us spend most of our days in a kind of creative denial of death. After all, why bemoan the obvious? On the other hand, why not be ready so that the obvious is less a surprise?

Sickness is a great preparation for death. You might call it a dress rehearsal or the beginning of our reconciliation with our body, which will fail us. When sick, we experience an exquisite kind of loneliness, even if surrounded with care and caretakers. People will ask us how we feel and we may even give them a number on that very useful scale for pain. Is it a one today or a nine? But the physical pain can be a one while the anxiety about the return of the pain is a nine. And why bother explaining such things after we have been sick for a while? It doesn't really help others to know or us to know that they know. There are many things we keep to ourselves and none so much as the persistence of pain and sickness in their mental and physical forms.

To use the dress rehearsal for its maximum good, it is useful to welcome sickness when it comes. Certainly we don't seek it or want it. Those who have "never been sick a day in their life" are likely to have a really hard time dying. They will not only die but also be surprised that they are dying. They will go into that "woulda, coulda" mode of anticipatory grief. I wished I could have been ready for now or thanked so and so for that or repented for this or that. Regret is different from grief. Grief is sad to see the time pass. Regret is grief at seeing the time pass, joined by bitterness. It is that sense of missing an important train.

A good definition for being unprepared for death is that you experience the shock of awareness that you have been alive a long time and haven't lived yet. Or missed the train you should have caught. Or that you are being lived rather than living, in Stephen

Covey's famous phrase. Or find yourself close to the end wishing you could have made up your mind about what you wanted to do. You may wind up saying with St. Paul, "The good that I would do I didn't and the evil that I would not do I did." This is a confession without an absolution. A well-prepared death may have dozens of confessions but it will also have dozens of absolutions. Reconciliation is the process of confession connecting to absolution. It is not just getting started on that process but completing that process before the door closes on the opportunity to do so. All of us will miss certain marks. Being prepared for death is the attempt to miss as few as possible.

If an unprepared death is missing what you might have had or known or done, a prepared death is more like target practice. It is not life as permanent bull's-eye so much as life as aiming. A brilliant art historian, Sarah Lewis, gave these words after watching an archery team practice. She noticed that they rarely hit the bull's-eye but they got closer and closer with more practice. Sickness is a practice for death. It is also a time to re-aim.

Sickness is also the blessed presence of a unique form of solitude. It is a time to lie down and let our unconscious take over our consciousness. It is a time to figure out where we are trying to go and to evaluate the steps we are taking to get there. Oddly, in the healthy mix of energetic hustle and bustle, we rarely get time to think. We are too busy doing things. Sickness un-busys us. Sickness re-aims us.

Lewis, who found a lot of wisdom in archery, concludes that a lot of us have target panic whether we know it or not. Target panic is that same anticipatory grief, which can become bitter resentment. When we fear that we are missing all the trains we should have caught, we often panic. Why not panic early and re-aim? Why not panic into "wishing we were dead" while being glad that we are not? Sickness is a dress rehearsal for target panic. It allows us to have target panic early enough to change our aim.

Many people find the blessing in sickness to be just this: the chance to refocus, re-aim, recalibrate. Doing that before we are on our deathbed is a real blessing. Lewis argues—in her TED Talk—that the trick to archery and to life is learning to enjoy a near win. When we get close to the target, even if we are not allowed to hit it, or if life gets stolen from us early, we learn the true meaning of those sometimes cynical words. "Don't let the perfect be the enemy of the good."

Duke Ellington said that his favorite song was always the next one. When we are sick, it is good to understand that mastery comes in the word "almost." Not in the word "incomplete."

When sick, we get to love ourselves especially. It is really us and the cancer, or us and the germ or us and the physical therapy. Nobody can activate our immune system but us. When we aim to love at least one thing more than we love ourselves, we attain a kind of immortality. You can still love justice or painting or gardening or your husband or your child while you are sick. That is what we mean by aim.

There is no problem in this world that we can't make worse. I hate to say something so truly blunt and possibly cynical, but it is true. We can make dying worse by not being ready for it. What follows is a simple guide to using the dress rehearsal well.

THE CURRICULUM FOR MAKING SICKNESS YOUR FRIEND

The first step is to learn to be scared stiff of inconsequentiality. A critic talking about the famous Ibsen play A Doll's House says that the heroine Nora comes to the realization that she is truly inconsequential. That she didn't matter. Sometimes sickness can show us the wonderful truth that we are not indispensable. So many of us falsely think that we are. But on a deeper level, sickness can thrust us into wondering what consequence we truly are or might yet have. Sickness will not stop your obligations—like paying bills, doing e-mails, or keeping up on whatever project the illness interrupted. It will make these tasks very difficult for you to do. You will have to live in another way than the ordinary. You will have to face a lost routine. You will be thrust into what you mean by consequential.

A second part of the curriculum of sickness is to learn the difference between wellness and cure. It will also pace the days of diminishment and face the challenge of preparing for death while you are trying to stay alive. Everybody will be sick sometime. It also acknowledges that everybody can be well all the time—whether sick or not. We can define wellness as faith, trust, and peace, whether or not our bodies are ill. We can define wellness as a place behind and before cure—and outline a plan for our time(s) of sickness so that we may be well during that time.

I frequently suggest to parishioners that they ritualize the time of their illness. They might review photo albums, listen to the music they love, write short notes to those who are taking care of them—all in an attempt to ritualize the time while sick as a way to be well. One woman I knew well was terribly ill for a long time with neuropathy that prevented her moving most days. Her goal was to read one psalm a day and to look at one page of her photo albums. She achieved it, and as a result, suffered much less than she might have without an aim or a self-guided ritual. When sick, it is very important that we feel in charge of something. We may not be able to manage our bodies all the time but we can manage our spirits. Elie Wiesel, the famous Holocaust survivor, argued that meaning is here: you can't stop tragedy but you can manage your attitude toward it.

If we can free ourselves from preoccupation with cure and trade it for preoccupation with trust, we can arrive at the town of well. We can take seriously Jesus's statement, "Your faith has made you well." When we have faith, we are well, even if we are sick of body. When we have trust, we are well, even if we are obsessive and compulsive. Faith is wellness. Healing is the journey toward faithful wellness; it is a proactive strategy for lifelong wellness, even in the face of illness.

While sick and preparing for possible death, it is also important to be wary of miracles or denial or personal exceptionalism. People know that miracles do happen. One of the men in my congregation, Kevin, has lived with an active brain tumor and thirteen surgeries, eighteen rounds of chemo, and eleven rounds of radiation, for twelve years. He is a walking miracle. But miracles don't happen to everybody. They dare not be promised as they are unjust, antiscientific, antinature, and finally cruel. Why you and not him or her?

Miracles are also not very scriptural. There are very few miracle stories in "Q," the most original source of the scriptures, and only four in Mark, the first gospel to be recorded. What is amazing about the Marcan stories is Jesus's reluctance to heal and his interest in keeping the power ascribed to him quiet. He casts out demons in Mark 1:21–28; he heals a leper and a crippled man in 1:40–2:12 and gives sight to a blind man in 8:22–26. In each of these stories he advises the healed to be quiet about their healing. Jesus leaves abruptly after the healing occurs, again demonstrating a reluctance to show his power. He also begins to formulate his main healing message: "Your faith has made you well." Indeed Jesus transfers power to the healed from the healer. He says that we participate in our health. He says that we have done something right with regard to our health when we trust him. This message is in stark contrast to the finger wagging "what are you doing wrong today?" message of culture and context. Ah, you have stomach cancer because you ate too little fiber. Ah, you have a brain tumor because you didn't manage your stress. You know the health police and their punishmentalism. When we are really sick, even if we smoked and got lung cancer, it is very important to move to the land of trust out of the land of blame. It is very important to forgive ourselves and let Spirit forgive us for what we didn't do to stay healthier. It is most important to dive deep into the core of Spirit's unconditional love for us and our unconditioned love for Spirit. From there we have a chance to become well, even if not to heal. Wellness is different than cure or healing. It is the platform on which cure and healing and restoration can occur. But you can be well even when you are sick.

Yes, we have responsibility for our health. There are things we can do to maximize it and things we can do to minimize it. We do have responsibility. But trust is beyond blame and responsibility. It is the land that the Persian poet Rumi describes beyond the place where we are always hitting ourselves with a stick. It is the land beyond self-absorption. Rumi says, "There is a field beyond all this. Come, meet me there." Sickness is that invitation to the land of trust beyond the land of blame.

Jesus's constant remark after a healing story is to say "your faith has made you well." The cures ascribed to him may or may not last. Certainly the lepers had a moment of freedom from their leprosy or so the multitudes report. Jesus veers away from miracle on behalf of congratulation to the capacity to trust. That congratulation—your faith has made you well—indicates that wellness may actually be the capacity to trust. Wellness is not the absence of disease to Jesus, but the presence of trust. The best funeral ever comes as trust in the process of diminishment and dying increases. That trust brings the peace that passes understanding, which is present at more funerals and memorials than people imagine.

Of course it is most difficult to trust when your body has failed you. Even if it is something as small as plantar fasciitis, we feel a sense of failure. We hurt. We don't want to trust. At times like this, it is most important to trust. It is most important to abandon the life-tearing, caustic-making, stick-wagging self-punishments and to move into the room of grace and trust. Ironically, many people find it easier to trust in the midst of a life-threatening illness, when death really is nigh, than they do when the disease is shingles or something that requires the discipline of physical therapy. Both the small and the large disease are helped by the presence of ease. That ease can often come from a cold-hearted look at what it means to suffer and be in pain, joined by a warm-hearted appreciation that God/Spirit/Ultimate still loves you and won't descend with anything less than you can manage. That old folk wisdom is true. Many people get stronger the more their bodies fail them. They may not get physically stronger, but they do get emotionally and spiritually stronger.

Psalm 139:14 has a wonderful line: "I am fearfully and wonderfully made." Sometimes we find ourselves saying, "My get up and go has got up and went." People spend enormous amounts of time complaining about how old they feel. Some of them are just turning forty! Or we may have heard our grandparents complain about how "old age is not for sissies." I feel like every third person tells me that they are having a "midlife crisis." More than one person is looking for new energy. So many are just tired of being tired. And they are not talking about fossil fuel's replacement by solar and wind—although that would be great as well. We are looking for the spiritual power to endure our fear. Oddly, confronting our death, rather than fearing it, will work just fine to become a renewable energy.

We may be exaggerating when we say we feel like we are going to die because we have shingles or a perturbing cold. We may be exaggerating when we go cold at the fear of death because we are having chemo or have come down with multiple sclerosis. Sickness is a great warning sign. It tells us we are going to die. Sickness is an early warning system of the body's frailty. As such, it is during sickness that we get our college diploma in dying. We find out what frightens us the most. Is it not being able to be useful—

which also means that being useful is our core value? If being useful is our core value, we are going to have a very hard time getting old or dying. The time comes for just about everybody who lasts when they can no longer be useful. But they can still smile. They can still receive sunshine. They can still be an emotional source of positive energy and refuse to be a form of negative energy. What people really want is a little positive energy. No one needs any more dead wood around, grumbling about how dead it is. What people want is people who know how to be sick and to draw from a deeper well than usefulness.

Perhaps youth or beauty is our core value. When we are sick, we rarely remain attractive. As we age, most of us become less attractive, at least in social terms. Sickness is a great time to imagine our worth outside of youthfulness or beauty. Often the worst things that happen become the best things that happen because of the way we understand them.

Sickness is a great tutor. Its core curriculum is the development of core values. It teaches us what our consequence truly is and how we matter, if we matter. It clarifies the difference between wellness and trusting wellness, and cure and trusting the big fixes that are often so false.

The curriculum of wellness may also bring us to our knees. Sickness is also often an occasion to learn how to pray or meditate. We can pray or meditate our way to wellness, if not cure. We can go down to the well of being that belongs to everyone, even the paraplegic. From there we can emit and know trust as a form of wellness different and deeper than youth or beauty or virtue.

I am a big advocate of prayer as a renewable form of energy. Robert Frost says that a poem is a momentary stay against confusion. So is prayer. It stops the bleed. Simone Weil said that prayer is absolute unmixed attention. What else would demand that better than our own end?

Many of us imagine that we don't have time to attend to large matters and we fear that our lives are being eaten up by the small. Sickness is a great time to learn to meditate. We can learn meditation and become an imperfectionist about it. Don't try to do it right. Just sit down and empty your mind for a few minutes an hour and allow yourself to be searched, instead of searching. Spirit will breeze in to the empty space and alert you to something you don't already know.

Being well while sick also involves getting free of self-blame. What we want to avoid at the end of life is a confession without an absolution. When we get stuck in self-blame, we are refusing the extraordinary grace of forgiveness. Being fully forgiven, not completely perfect, is very much the meaning of life. Why not aim for that? It often involves the gift of looking straight at death in such a way as to tap the core of basic trust and basic grace. Again, ironically, those who have never been sick are usually pretty bad at their first sickness. They panic. They don't know what is renewing. They are "afraid of death" in that untutored way that a child is afraid of being tested. Adults know that being tested is good muscle building. Sickness is good spiritual muscle building. It practices us for diminishment. A child who has never failed until twenty-nine is going to have a really hard time with failure. A child who has survived a few brushes and bruises will do much better. An adult who suddenly gets sick at seventy is going to have a very hard time being sick. They won't be practiced at diminishment or aware of the gifts that it brings.

A father tells the story of his son at Thanksgiving. It was the first year that the family was gathering at the son's instead of the father's house. The son's grandmother and father's mother was the senior at the table. Someone said that stuffing should no longer be put in the turkey because it was potentially unhealthy. The grandmother went off. She puttered and spewed and took the opportunity to tell everyone that she was more than a little sick of new ideas. The conversation deteriorated. People left the table with a form of spiritual indigestion. Later in the afternoon, the son came to the father and put his hands on his father's shoulders and said, "Dad, it's not your fault." Often at the end of our lives, we are looking for something very simple, like a blessing, or a handshake or a touch. The story of death that is usually told is that of a big showdown with an angry God. Instead, death is sometimes a relief, a sense of blessing and knowledge that "it is not our fault," but instead "it" was our privilege.

If, when we get sick, we find ourselves blaming ourselves for being sick, we are learning something very important about who we are. We were probably also blaming ourselves for matters when we were well. Is blame a way to live? Especially when there are so many other more renewing options. You could instead imagine yourself part of a great system, a great family, a rapidly changing culture. You could learn to appreciate the chaos around how to properly cook a turkey or unhealthy habits and the way they are hard to wiggle out of. You could wonder about the point of your life. Is it just to avoid criticism? Or is there something you need to love so much that you can do it whether you are sick or well? Can't you just be happy with almost and the near win that most of our lives are?

Death often knocks on our door in an emotional form of sickness, the kind that surely does follow physical sickness around. We become mean to ourselves rather than generous to ourselves when sick, even though we wouldn't treat our sick dog that way. The dog we would bring a fresh blanket, special food, and tender words. Most humans will find humans who will do that as well. What is odd is that we don't offer sickness specialing to ourselves.

When sick, we have the chance to imagine other realities, worlds in which we are not in control but instead out of control; worlds in which we are not in charge but instead in need of help. We get to receive and get off the giving, giving, giving—which actually drives many of us crazy in the first place, whether we will admit it or not. The curriculum of reconciliation to sickness is so simple that it can be the hardest course we ever take. We finally get beyond following the orders to be joyful or happy or blessed all the time. Sickness is no fun. Bad feelings are natural. When sick, we are sick. Adding confusion and a sense that we are doing sickness "wrong" or "inadequately" doesn't help. Sickness is a rehearsal for our end. We may as well participate fully in it.

A GOOD WORD FOR MEMORIZING SCRIPTURE

As a child, I was forced to memorize scripture. I went to a Missouri Synod parochial school where we had confirmation the first hour and Bible the second hour. Then we got to the less important subjects for the rest of the day.

I liked it. I only came to dislike it later, when I found out that people belted the Bible. I didn't know that some Christians did Bible "swords," calling out Bible verses to see who was most versed in the verses. I didn't know that these contests were designed to call out the spiritually dumb or numb. My teachers were on the kind side of memorization. They gave us these lessons as a gift, not an obligation. Their grace graced me. I like what I know of scripture verses. I feel more capable because I have a mind full of good words.

I have discovered that my memories of scripture are helpful, whether the Baptists practice sword or the Lutherans require. When I had a mastectomy, I recited scripture on the way in and out of surgery. I used the 23rd Psalm and was able to assure myself that even if I walked through the valley of death, I need fear no evil. I also remembered that great verse from Isaiah 43:1, "When you pass through the waters . . . I will be with you. The waters will not overwhelm you."

When a drunk driver hit me, I recited scripture all the way in the ambulance and while in a full body cast. When an eight-point buck hit my car, and an antler ended up in my lap, next to the air bag, I recited scripture. "God is our refuge and strength, a very present help in trouble. Therefore we will not fear, though the earth shake or the mountains tumble into the sea" (Psalm 46).

You get the drift. Rituals can help us through crisis. You don't have to be a Christian to memorize scripture. You can also memorize poetry or the Koran or the Torah.

Memorization is not getting every word right. It is remembering the meaning behind the words. It is being comforted by the presence of God, through words. You could call my ambulance spirituality simplistic or literalistic or both. That would be fair. But there is a repository in a child that matters. I also had a glow-in-the-dark plastic cross but let's leave that alone for now.

I want to advocate some early memorization of some scriptures for three reasons.

One is the extraordinary apocalyptic nature of the times. Just look at the movies. One after another puts hunger into what should be childish games.

Second is the need for ritual. We don't pray much at table; we don't worship in rote ways. We don't have many words that we say over and over again. Repeated words, like those in hymns, are very helpful to people under and in the grip of chaos.

The third is either named Shakespeare or sly antidotes to the computer's assault on our memory. Many parents worry that their children are too hooked on the computer. The reason, as Piaget would be glad to tell you, is that the parents are hooked on the computer and the children are just imitating them. I am less worried about kids and "screen time" than most parents are. But I am worried about what happens to my memory as the robot takes it over. Plus, what if I lose my computer or forget to charge it? What do I have that is mine when my robot is not with me?

A new book advocating that we teach children to memorize Shakespeare says that memorization makes you feel capable. Written by Ken Ludwig and titled *How to Teach Your Children Shakespeare*, it lets scholarship dance around with fun.

How do we advocate memorization to children or the child within us? Let the kids catch you doing it. Turn it into a slight competition. Walk around your house with a verse that you are repeating or a Shakespearean sonnet that you are repeating. The kids will join in the fun. There is no need to use a sword.

There is a scene in one of the many World War II movies, *A Bridge Too Far*, in which an American soldier hunkers down with an Italian woman during a heavy bombing raid. They survive by reciting poetry. And what are scripture or Shakespeare if not poetry?

Memorization is too clumsy a word for this foxhole practice. A better word is the old-fashioned one, which is to learn something "by heart." We have also replaced the words "to hold dear" with the lesser word "believe," to our own peril and that of our children.

Learning some things by heart releases us from the gradual apocalypse, which we appear to be living. Thank you, Todd Gitlin, for that excellent phrase. Learning scripture by heart says that we hold it dear. It also slyly competes with the dominance of the robot by giving us something else that is interesting and fun to do with our time.

Plus, you capacitate your children with a way to combat insomnia and to be prepared to die. Why just count sheep when you can walk fearlessly through the valley of the shadow of death?

CONCLUSION

Sickness is a dress rehearsal for death. It allows us the time and space to become aware of our mortality and to reconcile with that fact. It has a curriculum best entered through our families and our folk cultures and absent that, a curriculum that can be learned and adopted in mid- or later life. We can memorize what was not nurtured in us as a spiritual practice. We can sign up to go to class in death and dying and not be afraid. We might even recognize that we need practice.

3

THE IMPORTANCE OF THE AFTERLIFE

George came back to his house yesterday, soon after I arrived. He is sleeping mostly. Diane is sleeping on the floor nearby; Bill spent the night sitting in the chair where I now am. I slept in Diane's bed for six hours. I hope Bill will sleep now on the couch, David is sleeping in the study. George has oxygen, a catheter, and pain medication. Hospice nurse came by last night, George's temp and BP were normal. He had two units of blood yesterday; Diane says his color is much better than yesterday. When awake, George does not talk but his eyes show he hears and knows us. I've moments of sudden sadness, no profound thoughts, but I am glad I am here, and grateful for all of you. Love Karen."

This e-mail is typical of those many of us receive at the end of life. His sister, Karen, is describing George here. Diane is his wife. David and Bill are his sons. George is lucky. He is not lucky to be dying at age sixty-four of a prostate cancer he could have treated but did not. He was one of those men who are somehow afraid of doctors and doctoring. By the time of this writing his family will have forgiven him this stubbornness. And he will be dead. When they take their shift at his side, they are thinking mostly of the before life. "Sitters" find that they remember extraordinary things about their time together. They will also begin to have thoughts about the afterlife. In this chapter I want to give these thoughts a context.

When I say the afterlife is important—as in the importance of the afterlife—I am not kidding. What is important is that you have a notion of it. Otherwise, absent a notion, you are plagued by a lot of silliness, both about time and about memory and about the future. You yourself will not know something important about what you think will happen to you, much less your loved ones. When you become a sitter, you will not only have thoughts of life and death. You will have thoughts about what's next. Where will George be when he is not here? You will want a notion of the next.

A notion is just that: a theory, a point of view, and a hunch. Nobody knows what happens after. Instead of being able to master the afterlife, we find that we enter its mystery, with a notion at our side. When we don't have a notion about something this important, we feel stupid. Death puts us surely out of control. We don't need self-flagellation at the same time.

First, why does it matter what we think about the afterlife? Isn't it just after? I think not. I think a lost sense of the afterlife has flattened time and given much too importance to our sixty-four years or so, or whatever, on earth. It has given permission to capitalism in its extreme forms to encourage us to overconsume. Not all of capitalism is wrong, but when it becomes too large and overtakes aspects of life that are not its realm, it can become very wrong. Capitalism flattens. I know the word "capitalism" bothers us as much as the word "death." It is just a system. You can use another word. But whatever word you choose, make sure it comprehends what has happened to time and eternity, both of which are flattened by the overimportance of the material and especially the overimportance of money. None of us needs another cheap political battle about political parties or words like "capitalism." What we do need is a way to cross boundaries of politics to find out why the world got flat and rituals got edged out and money intruded on way too much of ordinary living.

You may not want to indulge the politics of the material or the word "capitalism." Instead, push yourself to imagine what really matters to most people. Many people say, cynically, "it's all about the money," and they often mean it. Unfettered capitalism, as Pope Francis puts it, plunges us into the question of why not consume? Why not live for now as an isolated individual? Why not have just eulogies and not sermons at funeral services? There is no meaning beyond us and our choices to "buy it." That language is important: do we buy ideas or believe them? When you say, "I don't buy it," we mean we don't believe it. This language is one of thousands of examples of economic language invading moral territory. When I argue for the importance of some notion of the afterlife, I mean elbowing economic language and activity out of matters eternal and moral. How we spend our life is a moral and eternal matter, not just a question of what we do or don't buy. You don't have to oppose all of capitalism, or even oppose any of what capitalism might be, to keep it from framing any or all of your notions of life or the afterlife.

Unfettered capitalism has given us permission to put way too much emphasis on our personal life and way too little emphasis on the community or the earth or what Native Americans call the seven generations before us (our elders) and the seven generations after us (our children). Look again at George's tableau. He is surrounded by the generations. In an earlier time even more generations would have been there with him. They would have seen his life as theirs, in a context even deeper than that which George's family understands.

A high school teacher from Wellesley, Massachusetts, David McCullough Jr., gave a graduation speech that went viral on the subject of his book *You Are Not Special.* He is the parent of four children himself and says that he parents them for normal, not special. When we think about the afterlife, it is not about our list of accomplishments or the reasons we will be remembered or how much money we have or had in the bank. We can think about the afterlife as our communion with the earth, each other, and secondarily our accomplishments. McCullough argues, "Statistically, most of us need to be average." When we remove capitalism's tentacles from our most basic identities, we learn to be glad at our living, not our achieving. We enter into our years of life as well as the time before, which belonged to our ancestors, and the time after that, which will belong to our children, even if we didn't personally reproduce them.

The loss of a notion of the afterlife thrusts us into a sneaky depression. We lose a sense of our past and a sense of our future and struggle with whether life is meaningful or consequential. We become performance addicted as though life was one long SAT or credit card rating. We are not the first people to flatten life to the now, but we have become increasingly expert at it. Ancient people had other words for the flatness.

"Acedia" is an old-fashioned word for spiritual depression. It is a spiritual form of despair that resembles depression or melancholy. It is a radical form of self-possession, which is finally very sad. A notion of an afterlife lifts us up in this life and makes us less self-absorbed and less melancholic. People used to have existential despair about the possible inconsequentiality of their lives. Today we have that, because we are still human, and then we have the added burden of performance anxiety. Developing a sense of the afterlife can help with both.

The main question posed by the afterlife is this: were we consequential before we were alive? Did we matter then? I think yes. The Desert Fathers often argued that life's meaning is less our mark on it than its mark on us. We are part of long life, not just individual life. We don't know what happens before or after, only that by some genomic and mysterious juxtaposition we came into breath. Elongating our sense of life will help us live this life. Shortening it and flattening it will hurt us.

INCONSEQUENTIALITY, NOTHINGNESS, AND OTHER UNTHINKABLES

At a very important meeting of our "Growing Older Together" group at my church, about thirty people gather. We discuss all kinds of things about growing old. It is a precious Friday night once a month, an interaction of peers helping peers. We eat a sandwich we bring. And then we talk. More, we listen. We hear what other people think about their offspring as they age, or their memories as they age, or what kind of shared housing might be available. On this particular night, we were discussing death and dying. One very articulate member of the group said she couldn't possibly believe in an afterlife and actually thought it was absurd to think that there might be one. She was arguing the other side of my coin here. "Why would I matter that much?" The other side of the coin of overconsequentiality is its twin, underconsequentiality. We think we don't matter at all. Or we think we matter too much.

The leader of the group pressed her on what she meant. "If I am this small and didn't matter then and am plunged into nothingness, how can I matter now?" She went on to say to her own incredulity: "It is very hard to manage your own nonexistence." She led the group in her wry laughter. Of course it is hard to manage your own nonexistence. Her husband helped her out. He said he really wanted to die before she did. Why? Because who else would lay out Post-it notes telling him what to do for his day if she was gone. Yes, she has lived a life as a great manager of it. Death will not be kind to her unless she finds other verbs, beyond the one "to manage."

She made my argument but in a backward way. The worst thing about having no notion of the afterlife is that it thrusts us into inconsequentiality or worse, nothingness, especially if all we know is how to manage and direct and control. A terrible apocalyptic film argues that in a certain kind of end everything is gone, even the archives. To not be horrified or terrorized by that kind of idea is to be inhuman. There are other ways to manage the ordinary matter of death. There are other verbs. They are "to appreciate," "to wonder," "to not know." They are the verbs that open us to both life and its aftermath, to life and an afterlife. We appreciate that we are here. We wonder that we are here. We don't know why we are here. And we are glad we are here. The word "awesome" comes to mind.

If nothingness or inconsequentiality is your notion of the afterlife, face it. Stare straight at it. It will help you. Likely your defenses will prevent you from going too far into this black hole. But if your notion is nothing, befriend it. It will help you die. Those of us who differ may or may not have an angelic view of the afterlife either. (And we will surely never stop fighting about the word and reality of capitalism.) We may just be defending ourselves from nothingness. But as the folk sages say, "Denial is not just a river in Egypt." No one can claim to be right about the afterlife. There is no evidence. There is only conjecture. If nothing is your conjecture, own it. Just having a notion will help you go to your death.

ALTERNATIVE NOTIONS OF THE AFTERLIFE

Many resist thinking about the afterlife because they are afraid the conversation will descend into notions of heaven and hell, which are equally as preposterous or unknowable as the nothingness hypothesis. They are cartoon notions of the afterlife. Will you burn forever? Or consort with the angels forever? Neither is biblical but both have their advertising agencies. A remarkable number of people live their lives avoiding the afterlife of hell. We live in fear of punishment, both now and later. Punishing notions of the afterlife don't have much validity, religiously speaking. But they take up a lot of bandwidth in cultural conversations about "heaven" and "hell." To be kind, these conversations are about people practicing to die. They are playful attempts to get a metaphor for the unknowable. To be less kind, it would be helpful to sophisticate these conversations beyond metaphor into notions.

Jesus was actually unteaching about hell. He was proposing a vastly different understanding of the afterlife, in which God's grace gets the final word. God isn't on the throne condemning the poor for their poverty or the lustful for their lust. Instead Jesus says the final word for all, sinner and saint, will be grace. As one wag puts it, every saint has a past and every sinner has a future. Grace is a different notion of the afterlife than either heaven or hell. Grace implies a mysterious and universal safety and security, the root word of salvation. In grace as the afterlife, we name the direction of life as well. In the popular song "Amazing Grace," we say, "tis grace that brought me safe thus far, and grace will lead me home."

Many resist grace as a notion of the afterlife because they understand grace as reducing accountability. If all are saved, why bother being good? St. Paul often asked, "What then, shall we sin more so that grace may abound?" Grace actually is an energizer for virtue, not a warning. When we know that grace has brought us safe this far, we are propelled into virtue because we no longer live in fear. Grace fills us up, to overflowing gladness, and puts life into our life. It also is the destination or the afterlife and from there secures us. Christians understand that grace has the last word in the same way that it has the first word. When we live and die in a sense of grace, we find a source for virtue that passes understanding. We aren't "good" to earn heaven or "good" to avoid hell. Instead we are good because we are graced with goodness, even when and as we make mistakes or live lives less ably than we can. We are proud imperfectionists and make space for the errors of others as well. We wonder. We appreciate. We become comfortable with what we don't know. We move beyond the pragmatism that is such a good friend of the flattened world. We realize some things can't be bought or sold and that includes our salvation or final end. We move into a different economic system at times of death. We realize that there is value to human life that is not measurable or exchangeable.

Christians understand grace as the now life and the afterlife. Other religions have similar universal ideas about the afterlife. For Jews, Sheol was the place of rest for both the righteous and the wicked with no distinction. For Muslims the afterlife is likewise a place beyond punishment, where you can't earn salvation. For Buddhists, reincarnation helps you advance to a less encumbered self in the next world and the one after that. These notions may feel utterly simplistic. They are not. They seep into our daily imaginations and give us a point of view about how to wake up in the morning and how to go to sleep at night. Whatever your notion of the afterlife, my suggestion here is that you have one and that you understand such a notion as a great gift to your preparation for your own dying.

Alert: this is not easy in our culture. We do have a notion of the afterlife. It's just that the notion is that there isn't one. I repeated what my parishioner said on purpose. She is not alone in her fear of the nothing. What is exceptional about her is that she said it out loud. Many think that we live our allotted time and then we die. Nothing happens next, thrusting the now into way too much importance. That notion is hurting our living and will go on to hurt our dying.

There are many alternative notions about the afterlife. Many Jews establish an alternative culture to the American way of dying during the Jewish High Holy Days. Annually, Jews remind themselves that death can come at any time and that it is "OK" and "normal" for that to happen. Or consider *The Labyrinth of Solitude,* by Octavio Paz. "To the people of New York, Paris or London, Death is a word that is never pronounced because it burns the lips. The Mexican, however, frequents it, jokes about it, caresses it, sleeps with it, celebrates it because it is one of his favorite toys and most steadfast loves."

Dia de los Muertos is a cultural practice that brings the dead back, at least in memory and artistic form, so that the living may be reminded of their own death and less afraid of it.

Whether you are part of a culture that knows how to ritually embrace death or not, spiritual preparation for death involves making a decision about what is truly important in this life. If you don't have a culture formula or ritual, you may want to invent one. Such an invention involves a continuity of large time, not a diminishment of small time, to our own years on the earth. It involves a notion of mystery, not a sense of mastery or the excruciating pressure to be good or useful or to buy lots of things. This book very much wants us to control and master and spiritually prepare for our death. There is nothing wrong with mastery or control, unless they start to violate mystery and flatten life. Good things, like control and mastery, can often get too big for their britches.

Many people name their cars and befriend them in the naming. My friend, whose husband just died, has an old car named Carmine. Sadly, Carmine's engine blew a few weeks after J. died. M. made up the words "Carmine's place" for where J. had gone. She always said it affectionately. A ninety-two-year-old hero of mine named his scooter for Don Quixote's horse. You may get a larger notion or a smaller notion for what's next. My advocacy here is that you have one and name it, affectionately. My advocacy is that you play with what you don't know as much as you master and control it.

THE MEDICALIZED CONFLICT

When culture succeeds in convincing us that there is no afterlife, it puts extraordinary pressure on the action and method of dying. The medicalization of death and dying is a result of a lost sense of the afterlife or the ongoing continuous nature of life. If there is nothing "after," we better prolong our breath as long as possible.

Our culture thinks that death used to be a spiritual ordeal but now it is a technical failing. We've taken a domestic and religious event and mechanized and medicalized it.

Kate Butler, in an extraordinary article in the *Sun* magazine, April 2014, summarizes this situation. Her remarks come from her 2013 memoir, *Knocking on Heaven's Door: The Path to a Better Way of Death*. The medicalization of death is part of our culture's notion about death. It seeps into our spirits and we dread it but also don't have an arsenal to combat it. Medical care leaves the world of healing and becomes the world of bills. Yes, money really matters to those in the death and dying process. The dying person and their family are distracted from acts of healing or touch or final thoughts into the world of being able to pay for "care." If there is an afterlife of some kind, we need not be so delayed in our arrival at it. Absent an afterlife, very strange things start to happen. Intubation comes to mind: would we intubate a person so that the last moments are without words, just staring eyes? The frantic pace of an ICU seems particularly hostile to a calm or contemplative death that is leading somewhere, whether the somewhere is grace or Sheol or reincarnation. In the ICU there is nothing green. Often there aren't even windows, trivializing life to the patient and the patient's breath alone. If there is no afterlife, of course, we medically extend life as long as possible. If we have a notion, like "going home" or "joining the ancestors" or "joining our late mother or husband" or "becoming compost," we are much calmer, even if we are in the ICU.

Not all medical interventions are medicalized. It is very important to get a balanced point of view about medicine. It can help and it can hurt, if overdone. Like capitalism, it can get in the way if it gets too big for its britches. Two new medical programs have come about that help us embrace a sense of life's continuum with death. Palliative care is for a person with a chronic, incurable illness. It focuses on improving the quality of what life remains. Hospice care is the same but is more oriented toward the final days, where we promise to forgo all life-prolonging treatments. Hospice nurses are extraordinary in the way they fill up the spiritual vacuums of modern life. Each imagines a focus in lived time of three to six months and allows the mourners and the dying person a sense of order about the end. According to the *New England Journal of Medicine*, "Results are about the same as those receiving aggressive treatment."

During hospice care or long stays in the ICU, patients and sitters have a lot of unused and unusable time. Many report that they are going nuts by how slow time starts to go. Why not devote that time to caressing some notion of the afterlife? Such a meditation will help you.

PREPARATIONS: WHY WAIT UNTIL THE END TIME TO THINK ABOUT THE END TIME?

I encourage people to think of death as a five-year process, not a three-month process. You may be lucky enough not to have to think about your notion of the afterlife in the ICU, as your beloved lies dying. In a reimagination of how long it takes you to die, you have time to imagine where you are going. If you are lucky. Again, it doesn't matter if you are right in your notion of the afterlife. What is important is that you give yourself the gift of an idea about one. That idea will be worth its weight in gold as you take back your own power to die from the medicalization mischief. Why five years? Because it allows you to not be surprised and to engage in a process of dying, as opposed to living as though you weren't going to die. Five years is just a reconditioning, a stab at a number. Perhaps the number is one or three. It doesn't matter what the number is, as it doesn't matter what your notion is. What matters is taking back control from the medicalization and money mischief. What matters is living a dense life on many levels, instead of a flattened life, on a flat or arid plain.

We experiment with a notion of death as dying, not death as death. We reculture and recondition ourselves in a way of being and thinking about our own deaths, which keeps the intubators in their proper place. Intubation is just an example of one medicalization of death. There may be very good reasons to intubate. There also may not be. (I just had a parishioner come back from a very useful intubation after double pneumonia. It is not always the end.) What matters is that we think through the conditions under which we might want intubation. We are also dying before we are sick. That is the point.

Butler argues that when it comes to end of life care, "Nobody is in charge but the marketplace." There is a real conflict between our multiple religious traditions and those of many cultures and the way we die. Until we change the financial incentives, death will be scary. Changing the financial incentives involves a real inner ordeal. The financial incentives are real and the bills are real. Preparing for a way out of "money" alone is key to the dying person and to all of our preparation for it. You might even call it repentance. We have to repent our lost sense of an afterlife, which is the real spiritual power we have to die well. It is hard to find a person who thinks that medicine is what it should be, so involved are we in the question of prices for pills and panic at getting sick. We can't even get sick anymore without worrying about how much it will cost us. This is an infiltration of our souls, an internalized capitalism that probably won't change in our lifetime. That being said, we can change our own attitudes about death and learn to relax into at least parts of it, especially if we reframe what dying is. We can also change our own attitudes about health and its cost and be ready to take back our souls from the bill collectors. Dying is often something that takes a long time and doesn't really involve a doctor. Or better said, it involves a doctor but the doctor is not the central actor. We and that which we love and those whom we love are the stars of the play.

You will have partners around you who will be overly interested in your momentary life and not at all interested in your afterlife. Help them to know that you know or have a notion of the afterlife. Doctors will not want to discuss this matter, even though it is often the elephant in the room. They may even be aware of the depth of the medicalization of the subject of death and not know how to talk about the afterlife at all. We can note how deep the medicalized diminution of death occurred around the affordable care legislation. Some legislators tried to add a provision to the Affordable Care Act that would've paid doctors two hundred dollars to have end of life discussions with patients. The act's political opponents, who called it a death panel, distorted this and it was stripped from the bill. Why? People were afraid doctors would kill them by withdrawing care if they started to cost too much. Again, having a more fulsome sense of death and the dying process can assuage this kind of fear. Dying is also a spiritual process and not just a medical one. It involves a notion of the afterlife, which can assist the conversation about how much to spend to keep someone on this side of the life and death passage.

We will talk about the "talk" over and over in this book. It doesn't happen just once, but over and over, in different contexts, sometimes with doctors and sometimes after they have been excused from the room. Many new movements are encouraging people to "have the talk," and by the talk, they don't mean the sex ed one. They mean the end of life one. During that talk, we can dare have a conversation about the afterlife, which will fertilize our current living. It will also allow us to put in place boundaries around the medicalization of our own death. We may indeed want intubation and other medical assists. We may want the doctors to "do everything." And we may not. But absent a conversation about what we want and why we want what we want, our loved ones won't know what to do and we will be thrust into the hands of medicine. Medicine is a brilliant place and it can also be a flat place, unless we take charge of our notions about the afterlife.

It isn't only doctors who need to converse about our notion of the afterlife. There is also the matter of technology itself. We who love technology need to love it in such a way as to keep it in its place. I imagine that even more life-extending technologies will appear year after year. My brother had a stroke at age fifty-nine and was brought back from paralysis by a pill, a chemical, and an infusion. That miracle and medicine makes me very grateful. You don't need to dislike medicine to limit it and keep it in its proper place. To do that, nothing is as effective as the talk and the planning and the way they will place this life in a context of the afterlife. It was too soon for my brother to die. I could not be more grateful for what medicine could do to keep him on this side.

HAVING A HOLY LIFE, A HOLY DEATH, AND A HOLY AFTERLIFE

The goal is to have a holy death when that time comes. No one is keeping you from that but you. And only you can get on the path to a holy death. All you need to do is open your mouth and heart and ask the question: Where do I think I am going? How will I get there? That is the utter simplicity of the afterlife question. It is a pregnant conversation and opens us to eternity.

Even if we answer "nothing" or "nothingness" to the afterlife notion, even then we will find enormous release in telling someone else that is what we think. We will free ourselves from the land of the clichés of "passing on" or "crossing over" and find ourselves in honest relationship with those we love. That honest relationship will also refocus medical and legal decisions at the end of life. That focus will be life giving, even in the face of death and dying.

Dr. Elizabeth Kübler-Ross in her 1969 bestseller *On Death and Dying* theorized that dying people move through stages of denial, anger, bargaining, depression, and acceptance, although not necessarily in that order. Having the conversation about the afterlife will thrust you into these stages with enough time to get through them before you enter the active dying process. You deserve enough time to manage your dying well. Opening up the conversation gives you that time. Being prepared to bring up the question of the afterlife, early and often, with or without doctors, with loved ones is a matter of rehearsal. Practice talking about the afterlife and it will help you.

Alexander Huls says in "How Hollywood Killed Death," April 20, 2014, *New York Times Magazine*:

> No matter how much movies or comics depart into realities with superpowered beings, technologically advanced futures or fantastical worlds full of impossible creatures, they still need to do what all good stories should: Tell us something about being human. But most of today's movies are telling us that death doesn't matter. And it's hard to imagine a more inhuman observation than that.

Huls reviews a dozen movies and argues that they refuse to look at death because they don't think there is an afterlife. Clearly these movies have never stood at a bedside and wondered where their loved one was going.

One of the purposes of religion is to guide the living through the experience of death. Ironically, as religion "outsourced" its work to hospice nurses, in the same way we outsourced addiction to AA, we lost our main businesses. There is a sure relationship between the decline of religious participation and our lost function at the time of death. That being said, this is where we are. We are not headed toward the holy with all our resources. We are headed toward the unholy with responsibility for that confusion resting on our own shoulders.

As a religious person, I couldn't respect hospice more. There is no need to mourn the lost function. Instead, there is need to appreciate what hospice can do. When we talk about the way things might be, we might all hope for hospice for ourselves and those we love. Hospice often helps people with notions of the afterlife, even though it is supposed to "stay out" of the spiritual questions. Many nurses and doctors and especially hospice and palliative doctors and nurses disobey their orders. Ecumenism is a wonderful thing. It also keeps us quiet about the holy things. When we rehearse how to have our conversation about what's next, we need to help each other understand that we are not controlling the conversation or telling others the right way to think about the afterlife. That would be an insult to the great mystery of life and the fact that there are more versions of the holy than we have even yet imagined. As we say in my denomination, God is still speaking.

CONCLUSION

Hospice argues that there are five things you should say to a dying loved one: *thank you; I love you; please; forgive me; I forgive you and good-bye*. The good news is you can start saying the first four anytime. And the even better news is that you can add a discussion of the next to any conversation, whenever you choose to do so. It may surprise you how much the afterlife is a part of this life. Then again you may already have noticed and have begun your incorporation of the later into the now. You also don't have to wait to obey hospice orders until the end either. You can start the after, in the now.

4

EARLY DOTAGE, MID DOTAGE, AND LATE DOTAGE

Facing Facts with Freedom

Spiritual preparation for death is a lot like the Christian tradition of Advent. Every year is different. Children have one kind of Advent calendar. We open a door on a chocolate or a childish picture. As teenagers, we see time moving much less pointedly to the big day of Christmas. We still have anticipation, but we are also more able to wait. Our attention wanders to more places. Teenagers often enjoy a fleeting sense of immortality, a delightful youth, that lets them drive fast and not worry. Time changes in each season.

While we are in our child raising years or career building periods, we don't think too much about dying and death. We may be sure to get life insurance policies when our children are born but that nod to our endings is more for them than for us. Death preparations speed up as we age. Just recently I heard one of many gurus tell me to retire the word "retire." I agreed. He argued that the bonus decades, if we are lucky, from sixty to ninety or so, will have as many developmental stages and tasks as the earlier ones, if we but notice them. Here I make a rough division into ten-year periods, which will each have their own inner divisions into phases and stages.

In this chapter I am going to look at three periods of aging, loosely defined as our sixties, our seventies, and our eighties—or early, mid, and late dotage. Yes, people enter into late dotage at sixty and some enter early dotage at ninety. One of the challenges in writing a book about death preparation is that the audience is not fully identifiable. You may be reading now because you wonder what will happen to your partner or your mother as much as you wonder what will happen to you. When I speak of the different stages of dotage, I am not saying they will come to you or yours right on time. Instead, I am referring to averages and predictabilities.

Some years spring is late. Other years winter is severe. Sometimes summer comes abruptly. Sometimes you travel all the way to Italy for your son's world Frisbee tournament and it is rained out. Things happen. Seasons are not the same for everyone. Still, there are patterns: the way the iris follows the peonies and the day lilies come after that, unless the climate changes and shifts their order.

By sixty most people begin to be aware of bodily changes. We lose a bit of our grip. We find that our warts are growing hair. (Horrors!) We confess to a few senior moments and joke with our friends that we might have Alzheimer's. Increasingly, that joke has lost its humor: more and more people actually do get Alzheimer's, which apparently has a hundred-plus varieties. We live longer; therefore we have more time in which to lose our "minds." We find that steps bother our knees or the wrong chairs bother our backs. We see the gray hairs. Early dotage for most people, the time in our sixties, is a series of early warning signals about physical and mental weakness. We may simultaneously be psychologically and spiritually stronger, but the body has a way of announcing itself and moving the "wisdom" claims aside. We may be happier than ever and still wonder if we should be driving at night. By mid dotage, 70 percent of us have at least one physical ailment. We will have known cancer or heart valve problems or had a knee or hip replacement. By seventy, two out of three of us will have at least one chronic or repeating physical ailment. By late dotage, we may find ourselves off the tennis court and in the rocking chair. In our eighties, we will surely have "slowed down." Those lucky enough to make it to their nineties will have accumulated their aches and pains and likely be in some sort of supported or assisted living. It is the rare late dotage person who can live alone and safely—although I am on my way to the funeral of a vigorous ninety-three-year-old who was giving a ukulele concert in her nursing home three days ago. She was also (still) making up new words for old songs. "Down by the Riverside" had become "down by Shady Lane."

None of us is average. This chapter assumes we can't know if we are average or not and goes on to stake a claim for the hopeful possibility that we will know early, middle, and late periods. These may happen over two weeks or thirty years. The point of spiritual preparation is to make a bet on our likelihood of having different stages of aging. The word "dotage" is often used. I use it to add a bit of humor to the subject that is otherwise not very humorous. No matter how positive we are about the stages of our dotage, "old age is not for sissies." We will need just as much courage as we needed that first day in junior high school or on that first job. Dotage is an old-fashioned word: it means the inevitable time, what many used to think of as normal and now we tend to fear. Blame the culture of mobility and the way people live far from their forebears. Or blame modernity and postmodernity for its delightful gifts of diversity and freedom. Or blame a political economy that puts too much value on our usefulness and too little value on our relational capacity. Here I want to move beyond the blame and the whine about dotage and give it a makeover, a lift, a little lightness and preparation to its step. Most of this makeover is a makeunder: you will need to make choices about what to keep and what to let go. In dotage, you are no longer the keeper of what you once were. But you are still a keeper. Some of us may continue to be useful but that is not mandatory so much as optional, another choice we have the power, capacity, and desire to make.

Let me continue to undermine any sense of stages as simple or predictable. Statistics may tell you that you are going to be lucky enough to have a dotage if you don't die before sixty-five from something major, like cancer or heart disease or diabetes. But some people have a dotage that breaks the dotage rules. I just played tennis last year with a ninety-two-year-old and her partner. She and her seventy-year-old partner beat me (sixty-six then) and my sixty-year-old partner handily in three sets, 6–4, 6–5, and 6–3. People on the court stopped to stare and photograph the senior citizen as she cleaned our clock. I also know a ninety-two-year-old judge and a ninety-four-year-old therapist who have thriving practices. I have already mentioned my friend with the ukulele. I also have dear friends who died at age eighteen and at forty-two. When we prepare for death, it is very important to simultaneously have a sense of life's stages and the way some people aren't fit for them but instead for something different.

You will want to read this chapter with two things in mind: (1) that you and yours may be different, and (2) that it is just fine if you are not. Normal is good. Exceptional is good. There is no need to be uptight about either. There is a need to bring dotage back into the picture and into our expectations of life. There is a need to dethrone "usefulness" and to add other values, more suitable to people who need special can openers to open cans.

In this chapter, I want to mingle the normal and the exceptional. I also want to mingle the physical and the spiritual, the practical and the psychological. Because I am writing and you are reading a book that applies to EVERYONE and no one at the same time, the mingle matters. I have to keep repeating Ellen Goodman's great line: Death rates remain at 100 percent. Physical changes announce aging, and aging goes on to have spiritual and psychological impacts, which also have impacts. Think in a circle. Many of us rue the fact that we can't jog anymore or can't see as well at night. There is a subtle complaint about aging, as though it was something that was supposed to happen to someone else and not to us. We see the writing on the wall but figure it is not for us. If it is happening to us, especially if it happens abruptly or with great loss of motion or adaptability, we must have done something wrong. There appears to be no limit on shame and blame for people in our culture. If you don't believe me, listen to Brené Brown's 2010 TED Talk "The Power of Vulnerability," available through the TED website. Let her talk to you about shame, blame, and vulnerability.

If I were to advocate one and only one important spiritual preparation for death and dying, it would be here. You are normal. I am normal. Aging is normal. We may or may not age normally but aging itself is normal. As we age, there is no better choice than to join the human race. Accepting some new limitations (yes, youth has limitations as well) will delimit the limitations. They won't be taxed with worry but instead gathered into a full human life. You need not be ashamed to age.

My former boss is eighty-two. When I last saw him at a conference, he immediately said to me, "Donna, I know who you are but for the life of me, I can't remember how [I know you]." With a big grin on his face, he laughed and continued, "But I am glad to see you." We worked together for eight years, every day. I admired his candor. It gave me a great gift. I didn't have to wonder what was going on. He told me.

As we age, we can count on many subtle battles. We may think we are worrying about our knee operation but actually worrying about our mortality. Or we may be worrying about our mortality only to discover that it bothers us less than the knee operation. Matters mingle. In the guide that follows, I mingle both the physical and the spiritual, the normal and the exceptional.

If you don't believe matters mingle, just take one example. Consider the simple matter of our peers and how we compare ourselves to them. I personally went through the entire photo album of the class of 1969 from my college, comparing my weight gain to that of the other women and the men. I also took a good look at their outfits. I know I am not alone in this vexing peer envy and competition. In such comparisons, we see the matters mingling. We are not just worried about our health and weight or about our appearance or about our mortality. We are worried about how it compares to that of others. Of course, we look at the alumni magazines differently. We turn to the page for the class of 1965 and we also look at the obituaries more. We attend more funerals. As part of our preparation for the dotages, I often advise that we buy a good outfit for memorial and funeral services. I also wonder why we would compare ourselves negatively to our classmate who was "in such good shape" and died so young, giving us yet another good reason not to exercise. These comparisons, which are sometimes competitions, can really wear us down rather than build us up and release us to the tasks that are our own. I like my funeral ritual of wearing the same outfit. Wearing the same dress to "so many funerals" is a way of saying we know. We know we have entered a period of life where there are more good-byes than hellos. Every time we witness another friend or family member die, we become a little more alone. As Sharon Olds says in her great poem, "We move to the head of the line." We also review the matter of our own demise at other people's funerals, in their obituaries, and in the alumni magazine. These reviews mingle the spiritual and the physical, the exceptional and the normal. Here I recommend taking as many tutorials as you can.

In our dotage, we can either wear the black dress and frown a lot at what we have lost, or we can wear a colorful dress that says a big thank you to life. We may especially enjoy our old relationships and find ourselves repeating the phrase "We go way back," to the slight irritation of others who don't enjoy repetition as much as we do. At these tutorials, we will especially grieve those who know all our old stories if they die or become disabled or lose their memories of us and them. We can also enjoy them, even if we have to keep our happiness a quiet secret.

Again, there is a psychology to dotage as well as a physicality. They blend into preparation for death. The word that applies is "loss," which can either be a sad word or one imbued with joy. At least we had them or it or that. The turn into dotage has a lot to do with taking the detour around the town of regret. Think of it as the business route and spiritual preparation as the bypass, where the traffic is less and the views better. You can also have a much larger portion of the road to yourself on the bypass.

Spiritual preparation is wisdom. It is reality checking as a way of life. There is a spiritual preparation for dotage. It is the tool by which we manage the physical and psychological losses. It is blending psychology and physicality, body and mind. Spirit blends and assures you that you know you are dying. You see the signals. You took the tutorials. You got the degree in the subject for which there is no degree.

In New York City we just had a remarkable memorial service. Wynton Marsalis played the Woodlawn Cemetery. He played a huge free concert in the Bronx where Duke Ellington and many other jazz greats are buried. Marsalis shows a form of wisdom. We can regret that the greats and our friends are gone. Or we can celebrate their lives. We might even dance and sing on their— and our—graves. Jazz is as good a metaphor for the spiritual wisdom that mingles and blends as any. Jazz puts it together and then does variations on the theme. Spiritual preparation for death is always variations on the big themes of body and mind wearing out or down and the wisdom to see that as it happens, without losing a sense of joy, wisdom, and control.

EARLY DOTAGE

In this period of relative health, memory, brains, and knees, it is time to take care of business. I am going to name three key tasks that need spiritual and actual preparation.

They are retirement, "having the talk," and decluttering.

Retirement planning is urgent if you are not to lose all your money and your marbles dealing with insurance companies, who do intend to make money off of you and keep you stranded on 800 numbers as long as profitably possible. If you can afford long-term health insurance, by all means buy it. It isn't fair, it is expensive, the government and society and culture SHOULD have arranged things differently so that the elderly are not in financial difficulty at the same time they are in dotage. That did not happen. We are out to sea and have to prepare for ourselves. It used to be that "going out to pasture" meant that you still got to eat grass. It doesn't mean that anymore. If you cannot afford such additional insurances, which are profoundly unfair, go to one of dozens of social services organizations or municipal organizations or senior centers and GET HELP. Note where I put the capitals. YOU SHOULD GET HELP. Otherwise your dotages will become the victim of worry as well as all the other matters that are on their way.

Many of us have to go through a kind of grief period about the way retirement was supposed to be and the way it no longer is. We were raised to think that around sixty-five we would be offered a pension and Social Security and that we would quietly eat our supper and pay our bills. That world is gone. Those younger than we are being promised no such scenario. Many think that the government couldn't possibly be that cruel or couldn't possibly survive if it didn't provide for the elderly. Now that responsibility for "social" security has been transferred to the individual, there is a new day. It could be that for you, like others, going through a grief period about how things were supposed to be is important. Again, get help. Get a partner. Talk to people. Don't just stew. Stewing is even more dangerous than the failure to do retirement planning.

You need a retirement plan. You need to take a long hard look at what Social Security provides. You need to make sure that you are out of denial about money and retirement and security that is not really very social. You need to know that the majority of Americans have less than $100,000 for their retirement. With an average annual benefit of only $15,528, Social Security is quickly becoming an inadequate income replacement at retirement. Without a supplemental income, many individuals risk spending the later years of their lives in poverty, adding expenses to constrained working families, their offspring (if they have offspring), and requiring extra support from government at all levels. You may not like the plan you can afford or the one that advisors give you. The opposite is denial. You will know that you don't have enough and you won't know how to get it and you will add worry to dotage. That worry is not going to help you get to the Marsalis concert at Woodlawn.

The retirement plan should address the question of place. Do you want to age at home? Do you want to age in place, in a community? Do you want to move closer to your children? Do you want to move farther away from your children? You may not get to choose all or any of these things if you fall and break your hip and need to go into an assisted living center or a nursing home. Retirement planning includes a picture of your place. It shakes you down and up on the matter of a nursing home. Yes, they are depressing places if you allow them to depress you. I know a couple who still make love in the nursing home on Fridays when he visits. She has Alzheimer's and an extraordinary ability to enjoy her body and her husband's body. The nurses understand. I know people who enjoy the freedom of the nursing home because they don't have to be a burden on their families. I also know people who hate the confinement and the institutional smell of them. You need to talk with yourself, your pastor, your rabbi, your priest, your social worker, your daughter or son or best friend about your druthers here. Of course you would prefer to age in a place you like. Or be invited to live with your children or not be invited to live with your children. You may not be able to do so. I am not advocating that you get "over it." I am advocating that you get through it by thinking and praying and imagining your way through it. Through is better than over—and you may never have to do what you are willing to do. Retirement plans include pictures of finances, of places, of druthering—and they also know that we are not in control of all these things. I have several friends who still insist that we are going to live together in the end, with our own hired nurse, in the Susan B. Anthony Nursing Home. Only problem is that they want to be near their grandchildren and I want to be near mine and they don't live close to each other.

If you have a life partner, it is very important to realize that one of you will have one point of view on these matters, and the other, another. People are different and we age differently. A great way to have the talk with your partner is to enter by the romantic door. "If I die, who will you want to be with?" This is not a morbid question. It will bring you closer together. Many people assume the death of their partner will be the death of relationship for them. That may or may not be true, but it is emphatically not necessarily true. Having the talk opens up lots of chances for intimacy. I have a retirement plan in place if my husband dies before me. I will go to a church "home" where my friends are and my identity is. He does not yet have a plan for his future if I am no longer there. Many couples are partially prepared.

Retirement plans are a both/and kind of proposition. You can have a complete one or a partial one—and most definitely, you will have one that changes every three years or so. Why not? You will also change every three years or so.

You will want all your "stuff" around you in early dotage and later become uninterested. I have a small collection of scented geraniums. They are a strange plant. They like to be root-bound. They don't do well when put in the ground. If you put them in the ground, all they do is leaf. Put them in a pot and they flower. They like to circle their roots around each other in a tight ball. I have pungent peppermint and fragrant spice blooming now as I write. I'd like to keep them with me. And maybe I can and maybe I can't. But meditating on my love of these plants helps me look at the matter of place and aging and retirement with common sense as well as metaphoric lust for what I love. Why metaphoric? I am likely to outlive those geraniums. But green matters to me in a fundamental way. I don't want my last place to be sterile or without light, green, smell, and color.

When facing retirement planning, there are also psychological and spiritual questions. They rarely get the attention they deserve. Many of us think we are what we do. This "doing" is what I mean by being useful ongoing and our obsession with the matter of usefulness. It comes with the water that comes out of our cultural tap. One of my dear friends actually said to me, "You retire when you know you have lost your fastball." I never had a fastball, I am not a guy, and while I did play softball, I resent having masculine metaphors run my life, at my age. I also don't think productivity is the way to worthiness. I also think I am worthy of working even if I am not as quick or smart as I used to be.

Wrestling these questions of worthiness when "out to pasture" is an important part of retirement planning. If you don't have that fight before you retire, you will have it after you retire. Again this is not a matter of getting over but getting through. I may retire when I no longer have a "fastball." I join the human race in not just being a "giver" and an achiever. I am also a receiver and a sitter on a chair. Normal people sit on chairs in retirement; they are not all volunteering at the nursery school. Some are. But that volunteering is not their worth. All are worthy or so says every major religious theology. We are not worthy because we contribute. We contribute out of a deep sense of worthiness. Christians call that grace as opposed to merit.

A retirement plan will wrestle your money and your motives to the ground. Are you resisting a plan because you don't have the money or because you don't want to use the usefulness stamp that a paycheck brings to you? The retirement plan will ask first about how you matter and why you matter and then about what resources you need to "live." It will involve deep questions of how you feel about being dependent and how you feel about being "out to pasture." I personally love the idea of graceful grazing. I also have enough money in the bank to retire, or so I think. For those who do not, retirement planning is a very urgent and difficult proposition. But its urgency and difficulty only show how important it is.

You are going to be very busy in early dotage. You also need to have "the talk."

What is the talk? It is like that scary one many of us had with our parents and our children about sexuality. And it is more than that talk. It is a talk about the end of life rather than just the beginning. To avoid having the talk is just plain irresponsible. It isolates you from others and others from you. It refuses the chance at intimacy I have already described. As much as your kids will gripe about the talk in adolescence, they also love the fact

that somebody cares enough to have it. Your intimates will simi-
larly care. Having "the talk" is initially scary and ultimately secur-
ing. It is a path toward clarification and intimacy with those who
will outlast you. They want the talk as much as you do.

We had the talk with our three children after they canceled the
appointment to have it three times. Finally, we realized that our
denial about our endings was only half of theirs. Nevertheless and
still and all, we had the talk. We signed the living wills. We said
that we didn't want extraordinary measures. We showed them all
the passwords to the finances. A great relief ensued.

There are many ways to have the talk. Only you can know who
is supposed to have the talk with you. If you are alone, it may be a
neighbor or a doctor. If you are estranged from family, it may be
with a good friend. You may also decide, if alone, that you want to
go through the end alone. That will probably involve you in some
relationship with the state that you may or may not want. If the
latter is the case, you have the talk with yourself and the conversation is over. If you have a partner, you and your partner may not
agree immediately. But wouldn't it be nice to talk about your last
wishes, at least medically, if not financially and spiritually, with an
intimate BEFORE you are too sick to have the talk? Designating
your proxy at the time of medical impairment is one of the most
spiritual and responsible things you can do. It will take a lot out of
you and bring back even more into you.

Some people have a dinner party during which everybody talks
about their end of life wishes and fantasies. Others schedule a
family meeting. Still others find a long airplane ride gives them
the opportunity they had sought. Questions to cover during this
talk include wills, health care proxies, funeral or memorial plans,
disposition of property and valuables as well as gauging the level
of fear. Surely some honesty about Isaiah 43:1 would be helpful.
Do you think God was with you on your way through the birth
canal? Will God be with you when you cross the great river of

Jordan? Don't be afraid of metaphors. Sometimes they are all we have. Who is God to you? What metaphors for God help you? What if you find out that your loved one really doesn't have a sense of divine companionship? Will you think of this revelation as a crime or something you are glad to know? I strongly suggest the latter. Imagine helping your loved one feel less isolated rather than more at the time of death. That blessing is called intimacy. It does make parting and separation harder—and it also makes it easier.

I am working with a woman right now who lost her beloved of forty-four years to lung cancer. He had told me he wanted Psalm 46 at his funeral, which says "God is our refuge and strength, a very present help in trouble." He had also insisted that it not be more than an hour. She got the latter message but not the former. I assured her that she did not have to respect his wishes if she didn't like the psalm. She said, "Oh, no, we are going to do what he wants." That is a kind of respectful intimacy that is priceless.

The talk doesn't happen once and for all so much as it begins to pry open the subject. Recording the conversation can be very important—and assure that those speaking were heard and those listening were listening. Your mother may want your sister to have her diamond ring and your brother to have her dog and you to have her pearls. She may also change her mind. Don't diminish the importance of these "things" as vehicles for the spiritual. They can be acts of great love or great control or somewhere in between. Lawyers love to tell stories of how many people just never get around to writing a will. I wonder why.

A good way to open a conversation about death is to talk about the deaths you may have known together. My mother, age eighty-nine, still loves to talk about how her mother died and how good the funeral was. In fact, in general, asking about those who have preceded us is a great way to open any conversation. We often find ourselves living through these stories to find clarification of who we are, how we are different, and how we are the same from those who are gone. What I see most often is that people have the talk too late or after they are diminished. Such a talk diminishes the credibility of the decisions made and the power they have to secure and inform us. Having the talk while well is wellness producing. Having it when sick is sickness producing.

A retirement plan is a virtue. Having the talk is a virtue, especially as we enter our dotage. Finally, decluttering is crucial. If you ask people why they don't have a deeper relationship with God, most will tell you they don't have time. If you ask people why "their house is a mess," as so many say, they will tell you they don't have time. We live in a kind of time poverty, and some of us live in a time famine. We become the captive of the small and the trivial and the not put away when our entire spirit is begging to live large and significant and "put away." Clutter gets in our way of opening the spiritual channels that help us find our way to the bigger questions that our fastball and long-term-care insurances are keeping from us.

I live in two worlds and two kinds of time. In one, I cherish the minute it takes me to carry the compost to the composter. I get to walk through my garden. I get to see the birds, the sky, and feel the air. I live slowly. I live calmly. I am not pushed nor does anyone push me. I remember God in these times—as the one who brings me the calm and makes me glad for birds and sky and air. God nurtures me in these little trips, mostly because I could do them faster—and choose not to.

In my other world, I do not have time to take the compost to the composter. What I mean is I really don't have time for God. In this second world, I develop extensive "messy buildup," that memorable phrase of the children's book series *The Berenstain Bears*. Adults call this buildup "clutter": it is the mail we didn't sort yesterday, the clothes that aren't wearable because they need cleaning or mending, the list of phone calls not yet made. Not to mention the e-mail and its loud siren song. Or the things I can't find because they are buried under other things I can't find, or don't even know are there.

Decluttering is a great spiritual practice to prepare for the end of life. I have already mentioned my scented geraniums. When we declutter, we clear space for the things that we really love. We put them in the starring role. I often advise people to start very small in their relationship to their stuff. Throw five things away every day. Or give three things away every day. Practice relinquishment in some way. It will make that muscle strong. Life is two motions: one is getting, the other is giving. One is hauling stuff in the door; the other is hauling it out. This advice helps if you are thirty-five or sixty-five. If you bring in a new book, give away an old one. Everybody can make five decisions a day. And interestingly, the more we declutter, the more we enjoy giving things away. Start with the car or the office or the bedroom or the kitchen. Let the rest of the rooms worship King Clutter. Make some space that is like that clear day when we can see forever. You can even have a funeral in that clear space for things you love, like that bowl you haven't used since you went to Morocco or the scented geraniums. (God forbid.) The funeral can be fun, even funny, and a chance to recall what you are already forgetting and trying to remember by "object-ifying" your life.

I bought five glass discs in Portsmouth, New Hampshire, when we were on our way to Star Island, the UCC/Unitarian summer camp where our family went for a near decade and to which our children returned to work summers during college. It is indeed our interfaith family's spiritual home. The discs were beautiful, in green, pink, blue, yellow, and near white. Five of them for our five nuclear family members. When the first person dies among us, the discs will come down from their window. The discs will always be in whatever window I have close to me. I even know where they will go if I retire to Florida or Amherst or Fishkill. I have plans for those discs. They remind me that one of us will go first. I get to preexperience the grief and isolation. I get to imagine that we will not always be the same fivesome that we are now. Of course, that fivesome has already changed, adding daughter-in-laws and partners and grandchildren. I haven't managed all these changes well, to say the least. I should stare at my discs and the light that changes and moves through them more often.

Getting control of our physical environment can help us manage a more insidious type of clutter: mind clutter. In early dotage, we have important decisions to make. Decluttering and dedowdyizing can clear the brain, heart, and soul for retirement planning and the talk. If we are not clear, we will continue to circle back to the "little stuff" and condemn ourselves for doing so. Reenter blame and shame. Who needs them at the end of life or at any time of life?

Dotage is a great time for a "makeunder," which is also that promised "makeover." Many of us want to make the simple choices of our lives in more conscious, personally satisfying ways. We want to eat simply and live simply and to liberate ourselves from clutter.

Simple is actually simple. Better put, simplicity is when we declutter and let go of what has become complexity. Simplicity is a two-part motion: first we put away, give up, and then we take on. I call this two-part decluttering practice a makeunder. Once the makeunder is achieved, making over is simple. Why not redecorate your home with dotage in mind? Why not install railings before you need them or move to an apartment building with an elevator before you have to?

I think of the table in my living room. It now has a lamp, a bowl of papier-mâché pears, and two beautiful roosters on it. If one or two of those items were to exit the table, the table would be simplified and made more beautiful. Simplifiers and declutterers learn a new kind of math: less is more. The same subtraction applies to work life. To what can I say no today? I practice saying no to at least two requests for my time or energy by 2 p.m. every day. I measure myself by whether I meet this goal. I also open my time in more open space—and become aware of God's presence. That presence is full of grace, not obligation. We can and may make space for it. There is no must here. "Must" belongs to the world of shame and blame and obligation. Grace belongs to the world of the worthy and the free. Spiritual preparation for death travels the road of worthy and free, as often as it can and as well as it can. We don't perfectly plan for death. We imperfectly plan for death. The plan leads us to grace and freedom and away from shame, blame, and unfilled and unfillable obligations. Guess which way makes dying easier?

Closets, tables, and calendars are not the only places we find clutter. Today, with the eleventh commandment to be online and ever available, we have a new kind of emotional, spiritual, and physical clutter. I am not just talking about all the electrical cords or the constant fret about whether our cell phones are charged. Or where it is, a question asked with increasing anxiety and regularity. Nor the spiritual sluggishness that comes when we read the fortieth or four hundredth e-mail of the day or feel bombarded by information at every turn, from social media to streaming video to unending links to new information.

We are emotionally exhausted by the very connections that used to feed us. Connection is good; overconnection is exhausting. I worry about solitude, my old friend, time when I don't have to or want to connect. I also worry for overstimulation. Too much is actually *too much* in the same way that simple is simple.

Decluttering in technological ways is also very important to freeing the spirit in early dotage. We are becoming patterned to online lives that may or may not be good for us. They can be good if we control our patterns and not good if we don't. Decluttering is not just about old stuff and stale energy all around us. By stale energy, I mean things we don't need or want or use anymore. Sleeping in a house with a lot of stale energy can be very belittling for the soul. Sleeping in a house with active energy—which may include technology—is very good for the soul. Spiritual preparation for death is going to a gym for the soul. It is exercising the soul muscle. That soul muscle, if and as it strengthens, will take you all the way home, even if your knees go out.

I like the idea of a seventieth birthday party that knows we have done what we can when we could. Each of the steps I have mentioned here—retirement planning, the talk, and decluttering—helps you relax into the next period, knowing that your affairs are in something akin to order. Each task becomes more difficult, the more delayed. You will not be able to manage things as well at seventy-five or eighty-five as you can at sixty-five. Facing this fact with freedom and proactivity will make the next stages of dotage more satisfying.

In my ministerial practice, I find over and over that elders can become very insecure if they don't take care of business early. They become preoccupied with what they have not done and become the kind of sourpuss no one wants to be around. That includes their children and their friends. Isolation is a terrible problem for the elderly. They may still have all their "things" around them but usually the apartment or house is stuck in the 1950s, has a musty smell, and the person actually lives at a coffee table or a kitchen counter. Why increase isolation by becoming self-obsessed with things you could have managed earlier and differently?

Someone very close to me became a sourpuss. It was predictable. His father had done it before him. We all wondered if he would go the same way. And sure enough he did.

I write these words in hopes that you and I can avoid our dotage destination and sweeten rather than sour on our way out.

Nobody likes a grumpy old person, who can only talk about his aches and pains. By the way, these aches and pains are always a triple: they involve the aches and pains of the heart, the soul, and the body. It's never just one.

Before I start on middle and late dotage, let me put in a good word for control. I know people hate to be called control freaks. I wish I knew where that slur on people who control their own lives came from. Control is not freaky. It is fun. It is moral. It is a virtue. Authority is the ability to control ourselves, not others. When we control the things that we can control, we develop authority. When we don't control ourselves, others move in to do so. We become the victim of everybody else's advertisement. Or we become dependent on the state or our families or on the universe.

In the Hebrew understanding of tzedakah, the first task is to take care of us. Then those closest to us. Then our village. Then our tribe. Then those we don't know. And finally, those who will never know that we gave them a gift. This ascending order of morality sounds to some like the highest selfishness. It is exactly the opposite. It is the highest generosity, spiritually, to refrain from throwing yourself at the universe as a problem. From there you can accept help, if you need it. You will know in your heart that you have done everything you could. When dependency on others does come, as it will, you will not be ashamed to be dependent.

MID DOTAGE

I lust for this time of life. Grazing. Gracing. Release from long lists of obligations. No night meetings. Early dinners. Goofballing. Radical silliness. Flaneuring. Resting. Having fat dreams. Swimming. Playing tennis, after my knee operation. No need for a heavy calendar except for a small one with tiny dates. Watching grandchildren grow. Making elaborate meals. Getting to know my old friend solitude. And most of all, being ready to die without a sense that anybody owes me anything or I owe anybody anything more. Debt-free, you might say, and mostly in the spiritual way. Or you might call me the duty-free shop, if you wanted a joke. I also know that my lofty dreams and visions will probably not be fully achieved: I have been proving myself for so long, in so many ways, that I doubt I will just stop all of a sudden. I imagine that mid dotage will have the same "Donna" around as adolescence did. And I hope for just the slightest improvement. And I control for the maximal self I can be, spiritually, physically, and psychologically. Mid dotage is very much the time for self-control. If you can't now, when will you be able to?

My good friend always says to me that if I am not doing what I want to now, when will I? My eldest son keeps asking me an obnoxious question: what would you do if you could do anything you wanted to? Mid dotage and retirement will get to answer that question.

Feminist scholars have long known that something happens to girls as we come to adolescence. Carol Gilligan tells the great pizza story of a twelve-year-old girl ordering exactly the kind of pizza she prefers: anchovies, peppers, sausage, lots of cheese. At thirteen the same girl waits to order till she sees what others are having—and asks, "What are you going to have?" At fourteen the same girl often says, "I'll have what you are having." Loss of choice, narrative agency, freedom to be a self, in the way boys usually are, somehow disappears in the adolescent girl. I would prefer they keep it. It's a cut above. Not a strong preference, but I find people respond very well to this illustration. Blame culture and culturalization, and whatever you do, don't blame girls. They already think they are unworthy enough. When a woman gives to follow the rules or out of a compensatory sense of not being enough, the gift often sours her. When a woman gives out of a filled fountain, one that overflows with the psalm that promises an overflowing cup, the gift sweetens her and others. Mid dotage can be a time freed from obligation and pleasing, for women and for men.

Women, especially, need to be sure to both give and receive. To give from a full fountain not an empty well. We need replenishment in order to be plentiful. We don't need to give to others to be worthy. We are preworthy. We are already worthy. We are human beings who want to be less selfish than men. We sing in a different key, the key of the womb and the fountain.

For women as well as men, the issue is receiving God's love and grace as though it were ours. That is what is missing in our fountain. The issue is also self-care, which is such an ugly hyphenated word for such a wonderful idea. Self-care is generosity toward self and others simultaneously. It is the fountain in its cycle of filling and emptying, spouting and spraying.

Blame and shame seem to be what most people understand as their stories. I am going to offer another one. We are enough, as we are, where we are, even if we are failing to accomplish all the love in our womb.

We are worthy of ordering our own pizza. We are fountains that overflow. Women get to choose the life we want, and most of us will choose fountain and flowing, over and over again. I know that much of what I wrote here applies to men as well. I also know that it applies in different ways. The men I know are all different from each other and also have a commonality. They want to protect women. They want to provide for others. They are also more able to relax and theoretically mid dotage should be easier for them. I am not convinced. I encourage men to rewrite my section on mid dotage, using their own language. Why? Because one of the things I want to enjoy in mid dotage is speaking for myself and not so much for others. I want my life to be mine in harmony with others. The main way I know to achieve that agency and harmony is to not speak for others so much as I speak for myself—and order my own pizza.

LATE DOTAGE

I said at the beginning of this chapter that spiritual preparation for the dotages is a lot like the Christian Advent preparation. We open a door a day and never know what really is behind that door.

In many congregations, the sign-up sheet for the Christmas poinsettias is already up. Some will be memorial gifts, others just gifts. Some will be red, some pink, some white. When amassed, they will make for one of the familiar Christmas sights. Most will cost around ten dollars; some will be bought sacrificially, others from a full bank account. A flood of emotions will attend the flowers. And then a few weeks after Christmas, the custodian or the flower chair or both will throw them away.

Sometimes a scavenger, like me, will take them and hide them, hoping for the possibility of a rebloom. Or she will take them aside, empty their dirt into the garden, and be glad that another arrow was let against the inevitable withering and fading.

Often the "women's fellowship" is in charge of the lovelies, such as the poinsettias. Sometimes way too much attention is given to the lovelies and way little to the glory of the Lord. Still, and all, Advent begs us to prepare for the coming glory. We do it with flowers. We do it for fun. We do it for beauty.

Others prepare for the glory of the Lord through activism and fixing the universe, despite itself. Still others prepare for the inevitable glory of God's arrival as a baby with Advent calendars, opening small doors on large mysteries. I prepare by checking on last year's poinsettias, to see if they had the courage to bloom again.

Late dotage, like Christmas, is the time for gift giving. No matter how weak we are or how strong we are, the task is to recycle what matters to us. Whether we have male or female senses of obligation matters less than that we release the obligations. If we can't release them, then we should try to fulfill them with all that we have left. Most of us will die with mission unaccomplished. But in the trying and the releasing and the generating of a legacy for others to carry on when we can't, we will find the blessings of the end time.

We may not be able to give our big gifts in late dotage. We may not be able to fulfill what Erik Erikson calls the final generativity of life. But we can find a way to make room in our lives for an "other." To give a gift to someone—a daughter or a nurse or a home health aide or through a letter to our deceased friend's son—will prove that we are ready to die and be recycled.

The art of the last stage is to become less afraid of the wilting and the fading and still be able to understand us as grazing in grace, in a recycled way. It is time to rest and to dream. It is time to think of the "lovelies." It is time to assess whether we are done yet and if not done yet, find a listener and tell that person why. Release any sense of failure. Rejoice in every sense of accomplishment. Wanting to be useful won't go away; instead it will morph.

Simple things can help us in late dotage. Photo albums might need a glance. Music that mattered might need a review. Some of the most fun people have in assisted living or nursing homes is rock and roll Tuesday. Or when *Dirty Dancing* is the film of the week. Or chicken pot pie is the lunch. If we decluttered by giving away five things a day, we learned the virtue of small patterns. In late dotage, there is peace. There really is nothing more to accomplish that we could accomplish. We have cleared the decks. In that peace, small directed "actions" like one song or one album page or one poem could fill up all the space that needed filling. One of my friends has a spiritual practice of only saying the words that need saying. I think that is a version of the peace of late dotage. We can listen in late dotage and we don't need to speak. We could ask someone to read poems to us if we can't read. We could receive a gift and say thank you. Spiritual preparation for the dotages is designed to yield peace at the last.

There are people who prefer to reject this sense of peace. I give them at least an ear here. Obviously this is a different take on dotage. If we are spiritually prepared for death, we will welcome many points of view, not just the one in the book you happen to be reading.

CONCLUSION

All this talk about the different dotages can be confusing. It may even take you off the point of preparing spiritually for death. Peace can and does come to most people in the end. But it is not a pastel peace. It is hard won. It accumulates all the grief and loss that we have known and still know. It involves some self-management and some decision making. It is like a gardener's groan as well as a gardener's peace. It is like all that happens before the sweet ripe tomato is eaten as well as all that happens after the vine withers and is removed from the ground. Being afraid of the work of gardening can keep the fruits from ripening well. If you attend to the practical and spiritual tasks of the dotage times, you will find yourself richly rewarded at harvest time.

5

SPIRITUAL PREPARATION FOR DEATH

What you have done to practically prepare for death is actually spiritual. There is so little distinction between these two realms that it feels awkward to even write a chapter to distinguish them. The hymns you play at the service will tell what moves your spirit. The money you pay to the minister or the secular officiant will tell a lot about your spirit. Later in this book, I will argue for finding a spiritual home and having some sort of chaplain, clergy person, priest, imam, or rabbi to accompany you. For now, note the way the practical and the spiritual are married. They are simply two sides of the same coin, which is you.

From the spiritual side of the coin, we don't do what we must do or have to do. We do what we may do. We enter the realm of how things might be—beyond the conversation, beyond the hospice embrace. Here we refuse to think of ourselves as disposable and imagine ourselves as carrying meaning. The disposable notion applied to human life comes straight from the colonization of our cultured minds by capitalism. Once again as we enter the realm of meaning and of possibility, we have to begin with a decolonization. By decolonization, I mean getting the flat culture of "I donna know" out of our heads and engaging a richer, more prepared, and more vital culture into our heads and hearts.

Enter the plastic bottle. You may or may not know that plastic bottles have an afterlife. They congregate at the bottom of oceans, after they live a life that could have been lived as a glass or a cup, or more poetically, a vessel or a jar. There at the bottom of the ocean, they wreak havoc on fish and water, while suffering that hell that is reserved for those who prevail and are useless or empty or both. The truth of the matter is that nobody really needs a plastic bottle. They are an invention of late-stage capitalism and join the Styrofoam coffee cup and its plastic lid in being useful for the smallest speck of time. A vessel goes to shards and ends up in museums. A ceramic cup joins the user for so many mornings and afternoons that it has love rubbed into it. Plastic scientist and designer Sarah Kornfeld, a daughter of my congregation, tells us plastic is a post–World War II invention. Quoting her,

> It's really important for us to accept that plastic was created with the hope to remove the edges from the world after WW2—we wanted a world where nothing could break again and where nothing would shatter. The paradox is right in front of us—we created something in the face of war and horror that we thought could protect us from pain, glass, shards, and brokenness. To avoid a war with glass we have created a Shoah of ocean toxins.

Another scientist, Tasha Adkins, from the University of Vermont, tells me that we can't really study the plastic conglomerations below the ocean floor. We can only measure what comes to the surface. We imagine that eight times what we can see on the surface is below on the ocean floor as plastic tentacle ribbon. That would be twice the size of Texas. The oceans are becoming a chemical soup.

What both of these scientists tell us is that the problem of plastic is not just that it hurts the ocean but also that it encourages a disposable culture in general. It changes us to be surrounded by disposability. It is also easier to call someone white trash if plastic is the petty and putrid poetry of our existence. Ironically, things that don't die, like plastic, teach us to think we are disposable.

Disposability as a notion breaks the cycle of mentoring—which releases energy, increases energy, and explodes life into more life. Mentoring is actually a more modern term for what First Peoples mean by seven generation thinking. Mentoring, like parenting, also involves a lot of suffering along the way, as anyone who has been mentored or is mentoring knows. Mentoring is a cup filled with joy and sorrow. I used to be a plastic bottle and am hoping to become a vessel. That is another way of talking about the afterlife, that we who were a vessel biologically are now a vessel spiritually, for those we leave behind. When we enter the realm of the spiritual about our dying or that of those we love, we want to move toward vesseling and mentoring and away from disposability and nothingness.

I will now speak as a Christian. Christians believe in the resurrection. We celebrate it at Easter, along with the ubiquitous eggs, again another great vessel. Easter tells you that you are teachable, that someone can call you by name. You are not disposable. You are recyclable. You are resurrectable. There is a big difference between being disposable and unbreakable and being disposed and able to break, even to shatter.

To show you how Easter can function as a mentoring afterlife, I have to teach you about midrash, a form of reading ancient texts that lets you hear them, as though they knew your name. In midrash, a Jewish theological technique, you particularize the ancient story. In my denomination, we claim that "God is still speaking." This slogan in the United Church of Christ is not just a slogan. It is an entire theological viewpoint. It is yet another modern version of midrash. You imagine the competition between Peter and John as they run to the tomb, one getting there first, the other getting there second, one going into the tomb and then being followed by the other. You are talking about that day, the day of their race, as though it was your day today. And your race. When you write a eulogy, or someone writes one about you, you will discover that you are doing midrash. What did happen to me or her? What story must we tell about what happened to us?

Think about where you are right now. It is a few years before climate catastrophes become unbearable in human terms; a few years after terror took out a large building a mile or so from my writing desk. There is no better time than now to think about what comes next for us and for the planet. We are not disposable so much as learning to be disposed. We are learning to be good mentors by holding our past and our future together in an extraordinary tension, one that refuses to just be avant or just be old-fashioned, but to be both at the same time. We could call ourselves midrashians, those who honor their elders and release their young. Through midrash, we enter the world's story and the world's ocean and become part of it. Eulogies often capture this moment, but there is no reason to wait for them to tell your story, your way, with its meaning. That act alone will spiritually prepare you for death.

Don't get too high and mighty about stories. They are not "texts" so much as testimonies. A lot of what is going on at the corner bar is midrash. People have a few beers and start telling what happened during the day. They laugh. They cry. They share. They midrash.

Midrash is when you take the story into yourself and put yourself into the story. It is an ancient way of moving into the contemporary. It really is the only way you can be avant and contemporary, which is to find an ancient tradition to feed your inner fish. Midrash is the mentoring of sacred texts. You disciple them. You apprentice them. You reinterpret them—and if you are like any good mentee, you act as though your interpretation is much better than your mentor's interpretation. You get the most laughs at the bar. That is your job, to improve on the past. Your job is also to live your present.

A funeral, once composed, is a midrash on your life. A talk is a midrash on your life. Writing your obituary is a midrash. Deciding what you tell children about death is a midrash. Tribal cultures, like Christianity, which of course is just one of many, tell people the resurrection story so that people know what to do with children at the funeral of an adult.

Midrash knows that some years Passover and Easter are in the same week—and it remembers that the Easter characters are people who were observing Passover themselves. They had been at table on Thursday, saying the Passover blessings. They were there as disciples, apprentices, mentees. They were following a leader.

They were also resurrecting ancient texts. Or mentoring them. A text is resurrected when it turns you into a living vessel of it. What happens in the Passover story is that the people don't really have a leader. Moses has basically declared God's call to him absurd. He does not want to lead. He does not feel worthy. His entire answer to God is thanks but no thanks. Still Pharaoh is chasing the people. They don't know when the next plague will come. But still they find their feet, get them wet, and cross the river. It is in the MIDDLE of the river that they begin to sing their songs. Not on the other side. But as they are crossing. They sing not in the end when they are free, but they sing in the middle before they know that there will be another side. Their singing evokes the leader in themselves. You could actually argue that Moses's refusal to mentor became his capacity to mentor. The seas part, finally, in a reluctant or nearly leaderless leadership.

You may think that you are not worthy of God's call to story your life as well. But go ahead, get in the river and start talking. That talking will prepare you for meaning at the end, the kind of meaning that helps those who follow you carry on. The fact that you will die digitally is of a piece with the seas parting: there is a continuity in people and in time. Midrash explains and even caresses that.

Parenthetical peeve: I really wonder about people who like to say they are seeking spirituality. I'll bet they are not. God chose Moses and he refused. Many of us prefer refusal to midrash. To spiritually prepare for death, our job is simple. We have to accept the invitation to midrash. It is also very difficult. We have to prepare to cross the red sea. Sometimes the "I donna know" flat attitude is because we are afraid of pain and adventure. Why else would we stay this side of the great passage and waters of death?

BACK TO THE AFTERLIFE

Spiritual preparation for death is to ask for a blessing from the one who is dying. When the practical preparations are well done, the road is cleared for many blessings. Otherwise we distract ourselves from our feelings and our red sea crossings.

A man told me how numb he was about his father's death. "I just don't feel anything." His father had been very critical and very judgmental. He is the one who responded to his son's pleadings about how he was feeling, saying, "How do you turn this thing off?" The son thought he was referring to the monitor and its beeping. He was really talking about his son. He had frequently made fun of his son in public for talking too much. Even at his ninetieth birthday, as the son gave a eulogizing speech, the father said, "Get on with it." He wasn't joking either. What the son wants from the father is a blessing. He wants his father to say to him, "Go to heaven," not "Go to hell."

"Go to hell" is one of the better curses. You say it on the way out after a fight. You mean a big good-bye, not a little one. Once you have told someone to go to hell, it's pretty hard to get reacquainted. First of all, they never know when you're going to say it again. Plus you have given them eternal, not temporary, advice. Hell is a good curse word because it has a certain finality to it.

It is also a good curse because you can blame your use of it on theological misunderstanding. After all, no one knows where hell is. Or if hell is. Or whether you can get frequent flyer points on your way there. Or if it is cold like the cosmopolitan nothingness of superior existentialists or hot like the great fire of the brimstone bunch. Nor does anyone know if you are conscious of being in hell or whether your consciousness—so heavenly—is lost on the way down. Why send someone somewhere, even in a curse, if they won't know that they are there? What if they don't really suffer in hell when what you wanted is for them to suffer? Without consciousness, you can't really enter the Olympics of suffering because you can't find an audience for it. Is there Facebook in hell? How do we alert our friends "back home" about our whereabouts? Do they care? And do we care, once we are in hell, whether they know or not?

If someone gets upset that you cursed them with one of the better curses, you can just say you didn't know what you were saying, which of course is true. Even though we can't know, we have to wonder, along with some of the greatest literature and cartoons of all time. Red-tailed devils, pitchforks, and *Crime and Punishment* all come to mind.

I wonder who else is there? Hitler? My ex-husband? His lover? Nixon? My PhD advisor? Atheists only or agnostics also? What about the more Pauline sinners, those of us without a big drug or crime resume who neglected to do what we could have done or given a damn about what we could have given a damn about. By the way, "damn you" is also a good curse. It has the same virtues as "go to hell."

I also wonder about hell's location. Is it a one-way ticket or can you go round-trip? How is the food in hell? The pillows? That is a silly question, of course, because there are no pillows in hell. I can almost guarantee that. Oxymoronic, to put it mildly.

Curses, like anything else, have their strengths and weaknesses. When it comes to hell, I like to know that I don't know. Of course, what we don't know can kill us. Not knowing about hell doesn't absolve one from heading toward heaven or understanding that life is consequential and that what goes around does come around.

I also like to organize my life toward the very few things I can know. Go to heaven! There you will face similar questions but at least you will have exited with blessing and not curse.

Back to my father and son story. Neither may believe in any kind of afterlife. But there will be an afterlife. The father will die. The son will carry on. In order for the son to avoid the complex grief of unresolved relationship and worse, defining his own life in victim and victimized terms, this relationship will have to midrash itself. It will have to tell a story. The story can at least be the son begging for a blessing—a "go to heaven"—even if the father refuses. Spiritual meaning around death revolves around curses and blessings. Even if we did not get a blessing from those who have already died, we can give a blessing. And unfortunately or fortunately, the best way to get a blessing is to give one.

DYING "BAD" AND UNFORGIVEN

There is no doubt that Americans can be theologically divided around issues of heaven and hell, blessing and curse. There is a long stick down our spine about sin and forgiveness. Punishmentalism thrives as a religion in almost every denomination. Those who live to make sure they live in the right place later are one theological breed. They tend to be judgmental in this life as a result of their judgments about themselves and the next life. "If I do that, will I go to hell?" is a very real question to them. They actually feel the chill of their own mortality with that question. No one is exempt from that chill. People experience it in the night or in the shower, at the baseball stadium and sometimes even at church. But for some people the chill is transcendent and for others it is immanent. Either way you can't buy heaven or hell or know if you can get into one or the other. Faced with this existential, ontological ignorance, many assume that there may be a heaven, there may be a hell, and there may be a nothing. We then proceed to die, as we have lived, with a powerful uncertainty about what comes next. We may have an inner feeling or disposition toward feeling blamed or nonchalant or forgiven or that we need to be forgiven. Part of the story we tell in the talk and its midrash is to name this place. Do we need a blessing? Do we feel cursed? Spiritual preparation is knowing the answer to those questions for ourselves. If we are lucky, we will find someone to tell as well.

THE HINGE

If there is one hinge to your own theology of death, it is the matter of how large or small you imagine your personal life is. For me, my personal life is small compared to the web of my grandchildren, garden, congregation, and genome. Small does not mean unimportant. Small for me means more like penultimate, which is to say large but not ultimate. Therefore I do not care finally whether I live or die as long as I live to Jesus, as the scripture says. I prefer to live. I so much can't conceive of a fire and brimstone, judging God that I imagine my eternal life as more like a purgatory, one in which I will have even less consciousness than I have now. I find even the words "I do or do not believe in heaven or hell" absurd. Whether I believe in a heaven or hell matters even less to me than my own personal survival. My belief in God or the afterlife strikes me as a sneaky form of personal control over something, namely me, that matters much less than my fantasies about it. The hymns matter most to me: "I'm but a stranger here, heaven is my home." "We've got to cross over into Jordan." I have no doubt about whether there is another side. Since this side is so magnificent, I can only imagine the other is the same. Is it called heaven? Is it called hell? For me, it is called crossing, and I don't know what is on the other side.

METAPHOR RENEWAL PROGRAM

The metaphor of death as nothingness is surreptitiously at work in the environmental movement and in many of our lives. Many of us do not imagine an old-fashioned death. We have begun to imagine more a sense of extinction and nothingness, a toxic sea of plastic bottles, which we ourselves used and disposed. Not only might we not be here but no one will follow us either. The rival metaphor to death as extinction is renewability. Death is the normal way the planet moves some of us out on behalf of those to come.

Sloppy words and unmanaged metaphors have moved their furniture into our heads. Some call this the "cop in the head" or the "bishop in the head" problem. In this new death, we don't even get to die naturally or normally. "Nothingness" pervades. It is not like the French existential kind or even good old acedia. It is in the air and the water and the storms and their thunder, not to mention the movies.

Metaphors reimagine heaven and hell. Heaven is when you have a positive picture of your future. We wake in hope. Hell is when you contribute to your own demise, like an addict does, and don't think you have any way to stop making that payment on a future you don't want. We wake in despair. Surely some of us have been cursed by our parents, but more of us have been cursed by our participation in the disposability program.

In my metaphor recovery program, we stare straight at these metaphors. We acknowledge the new nothingness. We head toward heaven, while knowing we are in hell.

These questions are so large that they need a small door. The new big idea is that the new big idea is a small idea. Renewable is as powerful as extinction. It is just smaller and less self-aggrandized. Like the talk about death, it is small, next door, and mighty.

A really little and silly story may help, as it often does, when we try to talk about something big and beyond us. One afternoon I absurdly tried to save a chipmunk that my cat had caught. It is always astonishing how much better we are with animals dying than with people. People frequently euthanize dogs and cats in a way that they just won't touch with humans.

My beloved cat, "the Duchess," named for the county in which we live in the summer, replaced Hudson of seventeen years' purring fame. She is young and feisty. We are breaking her in; after all, she is a replacement cat. I so agonized the death of Hudson that I replaced her quickly. Hudson was a Maine Coon and Duchess is too. At the end Hudson was a bag of bones. Duchess is plump and has clear eyes. When I picture them, they remind me of how very different my legs were before the varicose veins appeared. They also remind me of a kind death. Hudson died a kind death. It had no nothingness to it but instead a something to it.

Note how I broke out of the extinction and nothing trap into a normal way of talking about death. Legs come, legs go, blessed be legs. Cats come, cats go, blessed be cats.

One Saturday in June I invited friends upstate to eat strawberries and whipped cream on scones. It was a delightfully simple party. We were outside. June was issuing its smells. The Hudson Valley is the place of my birth. I know what it smells like every day. My young legs and my old legs travel its paths. A soft breeze was blowing. One of us was on her second bowl. All of a sudden

Duchess paraded by, slowly, with a chipmunk dangling out of her mouth. She was proud. She was showing off.

All thoughts of strawberries fled. We even abandoned our whipped cream. I picked up a shovel, intent on chasing the cat, retrieving the chipmunk and bashing it to death. I figured that the cat had wounded it and was now just playing with it. Euthanasia was my objective.

Mercifully the chipmunk was alive and scooted off up the hill. I didn't have to kill it to put it out of its mystery. I mean misery. But, if I had, it would have died a normal death. It would not have the nothingness death. If we want to save our cats, our strawberries, our sense of cream in June, we need to normalize death. And head toward the heaven of a really different way of life.

We need to reclaim the normalcy of death and stop trying to fossil fuelize our way out of it. Nothing deaths fossilize us. They stop our history and throw us back to prehistory, the time of the fossil. In one generation and century we try to use up all the fossil's fuel. Normal death claims us for history. Normal death claims us for heaven, that time when we can even redeem the goodness of the fossil and not abuse it or wear it out.

WHAT LANGUAGE SHALL WE BORROW?

We have said that midrash and blessings assuage the agony of death. Language can help as well. What does it mean to pass? What does it mean to die? Is there a difference? The language we use for death should be as honest as possible. If we really believe that death is passing or passing over or crossing Jordan, that is how we should describe it. If we really believe that death is death, and that nothing happens after, we should talk about death as death. If we really believe that he has gone to his great reward, then we should use that language. When we have the talk with our intimates—or our pastor or priest—or both, we should say why we use the language that we do. There is nothing wrong with having a good solid hunch about what death is. We know we can't be right. But we can have an idea.

Take the example of beaches or barrier reefs. They aren't naturally permanent. They are naturally shifting. The parents at their favorite beach vacation may want to remember what they saw as children but their children don't. Their children want to experience the beach as what it is, not what it was. I was just on the Outer Cape for a splendid vacation, replete with large multigenerational tables in every restaurant. The joy was palpable. Watching the grandmothers stare at the grandchildren, as though they were saving sun for winter, made me happy. Hearing the children listen patiently to discussions about how many Wellfleet oysters there used to be made me happy too. At least they had manners. They had respect for other people's experiences. I heard them talking about how much sand the great storm Sandy had taken away. I also heard them talk about how nothing stays the same. They were unhiding death and becoming green. They were mentoring and midrashing each other in a grand display of how indispensable, not disposable, we are to each other.

One kind of person says they are seventy-five and don't need a teacher anymore. Another kind of person wakes up every day to bless something. Life can become intermission or impasse or it can become adventure, the adventure of midrashing and mentoring your dying. When dying, you are actually on your way to your greatest adventure, that of dying. I know someone who had a heart attack at eighty-five and moved into an 84-square-foot room that has 305 possessions in it. She counted them. She has a smile on her face and a blessing in her breast. She liked getting down to 305 things. Another woman, a sculptor, showed up at our church in Miami with a beautiful piece of hers. "Would you like this?" she said. You bet we would. It now adorns our baptismal and small chapel there. She was giving away fifty large pieces, for fun, for the fun of blessing and passing. People are different. Some have no story or blessing left in them. Others do. Spiritual preparation for death is figuring out who you want to be and engaging the adventure of becoming that spirit.

A lot of people think that Easter egg hunts are a cheap imitation of the real spiritual thing about Easter. Or they think talking about chipmunks in the same breath as ICU is trivializing. Or they think they have outgrown their religion. Or that there is no reason to get up in the morning. Or that you can't repent and just say yes, I was on the wrong track for a while. Of course they are wrong. We are all looking for an egg, a way through. We have to rid ourselves of so many zombie ideas, like that humans and nature are a separate matter, or that we have a right to plastic bottles. When we do, our stories get real and authentic blessing emerges.

RELEASE YOUR INNER IMMORTAL

When we lose a sense of the immortal, we lose more than a dusty old idea. We lose a sense of storied time. We lose a sense of beginning and end, and we float in a world where the devils easily have their way with us.

Capitalism, which is sometimes a devil that shows up uninvited, loves to assure you that the more you have in the totalitarian now, the better off you will be. Capitalism flattens. It makes the dense and the bubbly flat and one-dimensional. Spiritual preparation for death is multidimensional. In the flat culture, clutter and hoarding are major social problems for the elderly. Who would they be without the oppression of their stuff to name themselves? Why don't parents think they have time to eat dinner with their children? Or why do college students put up signs in bathrooms, "If you are overwhelmed with work and how much you have to do, call this hotline. Open from 10 p.m. till 3 a.m." This multigenerational anxiety is the result of capitalism's whip.

Not all of capitalism is a whip but enough is to warrant paying a lot of attention to the sources of angst about death.

Many of us think that we have to demonstrate "against" capitalism. I am not so sure. We might do better to pray for an improved sense of immortality. We might challenge the whips by imagining long time, not short time, eschatological time rather than discordant time. We might remember our great beginnings and our great ending.

I have spoken about the time famine before, that pervasive sense that we don't have enough time. Without a sense of immortality, indeed we don't have enough time. I have also spoken about the great release in "ashes to ashes, stardust to stardust" before. Not dust but stardust. If we regain even a little twinkle of a sense of immortality, we won't be as available to the whips of capitalism. Once we have flattened life to our 83.2 allotted years or 305 possessions, there is no reason not to have everything, do everything, and be everything. There is also no dimension, no before, no now, no after. There is just the horse galloping and gobbling. Spiritual preparation for death makes dense what is flat, makes multidimensional what is trying to be one-dimensional. Life is not just material. It is material plus. It is material and spiritual. It is multidimensional. When we spiritually prepare for death, we have a big date with capitalism and help the material assume the proper place in our life.

Two experiences of late assure me that the broken time narrative is starting to really hurt us. It joins our fear that climate change will make an abrupt ending, to everything but the stardust. One is the joy our parishioners experience when we open the service, remembering the first peoples on our land. The service starts with these words: "Acknowledgment of First Peoples on this land: the Lenape tribe of Algonquin heritage and the

Unami-speaking Saphannikian Tribes." Begin to rethink death and dying as an eternal matter and much will become clear to you.

I told you about that subconscious slip that happened on Ash Wednesday. Instead of dusting each other with ashes and using the words "ashes to ashes, dust to dust," we offered stardust as our destination and our version of immortality. I have been astonished at the reception this simple twist has made in people's lives. It is simply adding the spiritual cosmos to the material earth. But perhaps that is finally "all" that spiritual preparation for death really is.

We need a credible sense of immortality in order to manage the time famine. When we have a sense of long time and unending time, we are less likely to scrunch everything into today. Instead we can deepen the always and the everyday, like washing dishes or flossing teeth, or any joining of spirit to flesh. We can infuse trust into managing and administering. We can be less rushed in our 83.2 years. When we sense the sacred in our ashes and our stardust, consumerism is less the default position for spending our time. The time famine is no longer allowed to be an active degradation of everyday life.

Many people don't have the choices we need to sacralize our time. I think of the awful choices online or the ways we are made stupid by doing our own taxes. Why can't taxation be simpler? Or the new health insurance coverage comprehensible? How many choices can a person face and not become overwhelmed? Can I afford it? Or not? Does anybody really know how to read his or her gas or electric bills? How do I break through the computerized phone system and talk with a real person? How can I avoid payday scams? If I talk to my kid's teacher, is there any chance she has the freedom of mind to hear me? How do I not explode when my boss harasses me? If I go to the emergency room, is that overly stressed nurse really going to be able to help me? How can

I be polite when I get fundraising calls at dinner? Is everybody really trying to scam everybody else all the time? These are all forms of capitalism gone vinegar.

CONCLUSION

Very few of us see the divine in these dilemmas. We will find the energy to turn the vinegar back to wine when we accept the Easter gift to imagine long time, resurrected time, and stardust all around us. In that shift, we will find that we are spiritually prepared for death . . . and life.

6

SPIRITUAL AND PRACTICAL COMBINED

Last week at a Metropolitan Community Church in Florida I took communion for probably the umpteenth time in my life. I have even received it from Roman Catholic nuns before. But I never heard the words of institution said like this: "Jesus sat at table with his disciples and after the meal was over, he gathered the crumbs of bread left at the table, blessed the crumbs, and gave them to his disciples, saying 'Remember me.'" This change of words kind of threw me. He picked up crumbs? What an interesting idea. Instead of communion happening with a whole piece or loaf of bread, which is broken (a bread that usually has been prepared in my tradition by a deacon with a cut down the middle so there is ease of breaking), was communion done with crumbs? I was enchanted by the idea. It helped me through many moments. If Jesus could pick up the crumbs and if his bread wasn't whole, is it all right to alter a ritual? We alter it all the time, often at the altar. Communion is a spiritual practice. It doesn't have to be done right. When it comes to linking the spiritual and the practical at the time of death and as we approach death, maybe we need a strategy of crumbs. Perhaps we need a perpetually altering practice as we approach different altars. Here I want to argue that we are going to have many occasions to alter at the altar. Here, as we prepare for death or find its knock on our door, we need permission to develop spiritual practices.

A spiritual practice picks up the fragments and blesses them. A spiritual practice stops complaining about the administration it takes to manage everyday life and starts being blessed by it, infusing trust into it, imagining that community comes from good administration and isolation comes from its absence. Often we add to the grief we feel by not having homemade rituals with which to sustain it. A ritual might be like the one many of us use on phone calls at the end. "I love you," we will say. Or the post-9/11 version, "Be safe." Rituals can be as homemade as pie. A ritual is a spiritual practice. Instead of just eating, we imagine a holy meal. Instead of just saying good-bye and hanging up the phone, we add love or a blessing. Instead of just turning off the lights at the bedside of someone in hospice or hospital, we turn them off with the knowledge that the lights may be going off permanently for the person whom we are loving. Eventually they will also go off for us.

A spiritual practice does what you can when you should have done it. Not after you should have done it. Lent may cause you to give up doughnuts, but it also drives you to a deeper relinquishment, early enough for it to be just and to matter. As I mentioned earlier, Todd Gitlin says we are in a slow-motion apocalypse regarding climate change. He is right. A spiritual practice knows that it knows that. It comprehends. It goes solar, knowing it can't afford not to. A spiritual practice looks at the ordinary as though it was extraordinary. A spiritual practice takes the practical and practices turning it into something just a bit more. A spiritual practice alerts us that the holy is lurking. It says that God is in this place, or the holy or the deep is in this place, and we did not know it. A spiritual practice resacralizes the desacralized. Because we have lost so many folk traditions, we often find ourselves strangely numb at the time of death. No one is keeping us from resacralizing the desacralized, even if we don't believe in God but are "spiritual if not religious." No one keeps us from the pause that prays or at least thinks about what is happening right before our very eyes.

I will give an example that is outside the realm of death. One morning I woke up again realizing I hadn't made my dish for the Oscars potluck I was going to that night. The invitation came with orders: we are to bring a dish that comes out of one of the movies. I am to be clever, erudite, and also a good cook. It will be a fancy party and I won't have the right clothes or the right dish or know how to make the right conversation. I was having some social anxiety about my dish. Actually I was having existential anxiety about my place in the universe. I just let the dish carry it. I don't even know what all the movies are, much less what to make. So I started throwing something at a pot and all of a sudden I started having fun with it. I did have some red pepper flakes that were a favor left over from another high-end party, where I was also out of my place. I did have some vegetable broth. There were those dappled beans that had been in that jar for way too long. And yes, we had venison in our freezer. All of a sudden a chili developed that will have to find a reason, in the conversation, for existing. A fragment dish, I'll call it. From a chore, making the chili turned out to be fun. That is a spiritual practice: a deepening of supper through dinner to dining. I won't be the only person at the party wondering if her offering is worthy, existentially and practically. I think I will call it what Captain Phillips wished he had to eat, while starving. Yes, *Captain Phillips* was a movie up for an Oscar. But I didn't know it then. I found out as I turned my cooking from performance to play.

In a spiritual practice, we will be obeying Wendell Berry's great rule: be joyful, even though you have considered all the facts. You will be obeying the spiritual orders to throw an anchor into the future you want to build and pulling yourself along by its chain.

Spiritual practices are a pause at the door of the dying: we may not see her again. They are a ritualized language that we say each time we greet and each time we depart. They may involve a nickname, the way people name a car they love. "How are things at the Waldorf today?" we may ask in the ICU. "No dancing tonight." "How was the three-star meal?" These are trivial examples. They come from the spirit of joy at knowing each other and emerge from the relationship we have with the dying. We can also instruct people in how to bid us a fond farewell, in the same way we can make chili out of social fear.

Sometimes an object will have to suffice for a ritual. I remember my own enjoyment of a glow-in-the-dark plastic cross that I had as a kid. I always thought it was so spiritual and it turns out that it was just a nightlight. The spiritual is a candle and it also likes to trick you. If there is a plug in the room for a nightlight, get one that is silly. It will help the passing. If there is a favorite sweater or scarf, bring it in and let its color be close by. If there is a photo that would cause gladness, bring it into the room where death is. Personalizing the sterile can be very spiritual and practical. Nurses may not like it. You can still show it from your bag and bring it and leave it. "Remember when you last wore this?" we can ask. We can also bring in a favorite food. Even if only a bite is eaten, that crumb will carry meaning and affiliation, love and maybe even laughter. The very act of baking a strawberry rhubarb pie can at least help us, even if our loved one can't eat a bite.

Spiritual practices are like an old farmhouse. You don't need an architect to build one. In *A Simpler Way of Life: Old Farmhouses of New York and New England,* by William Morgan, we learn that they were not built by architects but by stonemasons, carpenters, and other craftsmen or often by the farmers themselves. "Beauty is not ignored nor is it accentual but arrives through necessity." You can be practical and spiritual simultaneously by recognizing the necessity.

Someone just said, with a tremor in her voice, at the bedside of her dying husband, "We are out of nutmeg. How could that have happened?" Good question, right? Taking the tragedy and turning it into its smallest element is often a good way to practice being spiritual. The nutmeg question is about much more than the nutmeg. These questions come to those who practice being spiritual. They are pragmatic questions first and spiritual questions finally.

The spiritual practice of grief is not just for the season of dying, although it is particularly meaningful then. Pick up whatever fragment is following you around. It will lead you where you need to go. Spiritual practices may become a necessity at life's end and in the middle of grief, but there is no reason not to have developed a few before then. If my scented geraniums die before me or wear out before me or catch a disease before me, I will want to bid them a fond farewell. I will probably turn them into compost near Hudson's grave up the hill. They have given me such pleasure. And still, I will probably have to let them go someday. Practicing at loss is a good rehearsal for death.

A spiritual practice is not something you do in Lent or in church but instead something you recognize that you are already doing or wish you had been doing. Usually we become spiritual way too late, even though the opportunity to be spiritual is an ever-ready battery. Spiritual practices are more like solar energy than anything else. They shine. They are an energy that creates more energy. And like solar, many people think they can't afford the long-term investment. Thus we stick to electricity or Lent or Sundays or candles. And of course, these spiritual surrogates are terribly, dangerously wrong. Those who can't thank or relax or see will find somehow that they wish they had thanked or relaxed or seen. It's just a question of how the play is going to end, after the surprises of the second act.

Spiritual practices are usually something you should have done before you did. A spiritual practice resembles parents waking up in the middle of the night realizing they forgot to tuck their child in and rushing to do so. Standing above a sleeping child is often a magical experience. Because they "forgot" they were able to stand and remember. There is a danger in imagining that everything is normal instead of imagining that everything is special.

A spiritual practice has three characteristics. First it is a deepening of the always and the everyday. It is washing the dishes as though you liked to or flossing your teeth as though you loved your teeth, rather than just keeping the dentist from guilt-tripping you. Second, a spiritual practice is pretty much anything that tussles with the pragmatic and takes pragmatism into something deeper than its obvious and worthy utility. Practice is not the opposite of pragmatic so much as it's underwear, what you wear close to your skin.

You can wash the dishes spiritually if you also remember you are glad to have dishes. You can floss your teeth spiritually if you are grateful to have teeth. Spiritual practices don't war with pragmatism or pit the spirit against the flesh so much as they take the flesh and salt it with spirit.

A spiritual practice deepens the already and everyday, it joins spirit to the flesh, and it also makes you aware of what you thought you knew but forget. Or forgot. And forgot again.

Without some homemade rituals, made of the crumbs, you will find yourself in a deep worry. Spiritual practices take up the time that worry wants and also give you the energy you need to do the mountain of tasks that just became yours at the time of death. It is very hard to be the chief mourner and to keep a household or job going. Very, very hard. Ritualizing your life will actually save you time. Early and often you will need to make decisions about how much time you will spend being an intimate nurse or sitter at bedside. Some people want to be there "all the time." Other people cannot do that.

One of the main jobs I have as a pastor is setting up a schedule for sitters and mourners. Often we need to build a team and take turns and pay attention to make sure the chief mourner or mourners get time alone with the dying person. You will want to have discussed this pattern with your loved ones BEFORE it is you lying in the hospice or hospital bed or lying in your own living room. How much attention do you want? Do you want to be alone some of the time? Do you want to always be attended? These are very practical matters that carry spiritual meaning. Each of us is different. We say that we are introverts or extroverts and what we mean is that we need varying amounts of alone time.

Without direction and ritualized direction, worry will take up all the space and time you give it. Permit me to give you the practical reasons not to worry. It doesn't help. It wastes energy. Worry blocks positive energy. It quickly turns into sounding off, which is the opposite of the high art of complaining. Yes, the high art of complaining is a worthy pursuit. Many things are shoddy. Many things are not well made. Many things have become like the dead plastic that can no longer be cleaned. Complaint is worthy; worrying is often what keeps us from a good solid revolt against things as they are.

Permit me to give you all my excuses for worrying. I can't remember my passwords. I actually hate passwords. I was on hold with a bank that charged me $59 for an annual fee on a card I don't have. My offspring aren't happy. My partner is not happy. My hollyhocks have a disease. When we are faced with the crisis of death, all these ordinary reasons for worrying are multiplied. Worrying is the worst thing you can do at the time of death. Much better and more spiritual is to practically take charge of your time and your energy. Spiritual practices, like prayer, if you can pray, are a renewable energy, like wind or solar. They yield energy, which you will really need. Worry consumes energy, which you really don't need.

On the matter of prayer, imagine that you always pray at your steering wheel before you leave the hospital. Or pause there and put your head down and let the tears come if they want to. Or open all the windows and sit in the airy car. You might also pray with your beloved as you say good-bye. Or pause. Or put your head down and let the tears come. Or hug. Or give a foot massage. When worry about prayer takes the space that open-minded and open-hearted prayer might have had, energy depletes. You don't have to pray right, just as those nuns didn't have to commune right. If dealt crumbs, use crumbs.

Last rites are often very much on the minds of those in the hospital. Likewise, our best friend may become the night nurse or the woman who changes the bed. You can also have communion, with or without benefit of priestlike person, with a little bread and some cranberry juice. You don't even have to call it communion, but of course, if you want, you may. Some of my most profound life moments have been touching a feeding tube in a person with some wine I have smuggled into the hospital. Likewise I have baptized many infants who have died within hours. These old rituals still carry meaning for people who haven't been to church for years.

HOMEMADE RITUALS

These are some other homemade rituals you can use to help at the end. You will find some of them silly and some useful. You will also read what follows, realizing that there are a lot of different people in the world and what floats your boat won't float theirs and vice versa. You might even do them before you or your loved one dies.

When you are not able to sleep, pray for each person you love by name. Slowly. This is not counting sheep, so much as counting connections. Or pray the name of someone who is bothering you as you live through hard times. Pray that he or she may learn to be kinder to you. Just because one person is dying doesn't mean that dozens are not impacted. Pray for those who are impacted, like you. You may not be able to attend to your children while their father is dying. Pray for them. Pray for the nurses and the doctors and the cleaning people too. Don't think of any topic as too small or too large for prayer.

You may want to revert to a childhood prayer, like "Now I lay me down to sleep, I pray the Lord my soul to keep. If I should die before I wake, I pray the Lord my soul to take." If you prayed this prayer as a child, repray it from the point of view of all your birthdays. What did it say to you in different years?

Or pray to keep a smile in your voice when you speak, both to strangers and friends. Pray to trust love into your character and theirs. Make believe you are a great improvisational actor and that the play is yours. Be the person the staff is happy to see.

If you are just hearing about a terminal diagnosis, say to your partner, "Let's take the long way home." Touch her hand; invite him for a short walk. Take the long way back.

Hum a great hymn, like "Great Is Thy Faithfulness" till you've done it too long and it starts to drive you crazy. I am a big fan of humming. It is like chanting and gets us through long hours, peacefully.

Give out one hundred blessings a day, then be off duty.

Say a Kaddish or mourner's prayer on the date of every death you remember. Make a list for yourself. Don't let Facebook be in charge of your memory. Or if you like, teach it to be in charge of your memory. Either way, remember. Patterns of memory of those who are gone can be very useful at the time of active grief.

Daven or bow, as Jews do in prayer, while swimming. Or take a walk through the entire hospital and daven all the directions: north, east, south, west. Be sure to look out windows.

Use rosary beads or a tallit while praying. It is just knitting, which many do to relax. Relax into a meditative state, using an object. It is not a crutch; it is an ancient practice of using an object to help still the body.

Take your heart to the downtrodden. Understand the words "trodden down." Remove your boot. When you say "Others are a lot worse off than I am," mean it.

If the fickle finger of hate or fate has shown up in your life, unbend it. Massage it, whether it is yours or someone else's. Take the pointed finger and turn it into a soft touch.

If you have lost your grip, don't be around people who tell you to "get a grip." Be ready to pray your way into disability or aging or griplessness. Listen to God's love for your former and present level of grip. Don't be afraid of weakness at the time of mourning. Of course you are weak. Be very careful about being strong.

Remember what the poet calls the "idiosyncratic eloquence of an old apple tree bent out of shape by the weight of the fruit it has born." Allow yourself to be bent as an act of prayer. Realize that you are being bent. Imagine your bending as beautiful. Or listen to the old scripture, "A bruised reed God will not break. A dimly burning quench God will not put out." Isaiah 42:3. Find a verse and say it over and over. Take a walk with it in the hospital or around your yard, as a ritualized observance of it. Tell others what verse you are repeating. Chaplains and clergy often recite the 23rd Psalm at bedside. You'd be amazed how many people will say it with us.

There is an old and good joke about the chaplain who goes into the hospital room and asks the ailing patient if he minds if she prays. "If it will help you, Reverend, go ahead."

Prayer can be a very private matter. Test and test often whether you want to pray or the dying person wants to pray. If the answer is yes, by all means, pray. If it is no, bedside is no time for a conversion. Move into newer rituals. Clarence Jordan said you can't raise live chicks under dead chickens. Remember the future. Pray for the future. And don't force prayer. If it doesn't flow, it's not even really prayer.

When my son almost died at birth, I had to sing Easter hymns, all the verses, to him as they removed the respirator two months into his life. The whole ICU liked my weak voice. He survived. Some of their babies didn't. This is what I know of prayer.

Meditate hard on the question of the ashes. Try to become comfortable with the questions of the ashes. They can be very practical. Like who carries them out of the service. Or who carries them in. If you have never seen ashes before, these questions will freak you out. If you have seen ashes before, you won't be freaked out. These are good practical questions that have a spiritual depth in their rehearsal. The Japanese often clean out the crematorium by hand. They scoop up the ashes and make a ritual of it.

Your hospice nurse may suggest singing—as in hiring the newly popular Hospice Singers, who are now available for hire in many settings. Try to make sure you won't be afraid of singing because you will have sung songs before.

You may also find your creativity released around death. One person I know created a Moses boat for his beloved's ashes. The beloved was a child. The ritual was gorgeous. It showed that the bereaved was not afraid of death, even though the death had been a horrific one.

You may want to ritualize your life before your death or dying. Consider this: in 2002, for his play *The Last Supper*, Arthur Schmidt invited viewers to the Brooklyn house where he was then living, to watch him make dinner as he talked about faith and the players at Jesus's table during his final meal. Now, with *My Last*

Play, Schmidt is performing—well, his last play. In it, he talks about his life on the margins of the American theater. Then he invites each audience member to choose a theater book to take from his library of two thousand: the play will run until there are no books left.

I like the way Schmidt is valuing his life and his art. He is also understanding his "speckness." I like to use the words, "I am but a speck of time and matter." Earth is four and a half billion years old. The rocks in your backyard are moving, if only you could stand still enough to watch. Being a speck is the spiritual meaning of death. Standing in awe at that speck and its possessions is also the spiritual meaning of death. In a ritual, we connect all those books on our shelves to all that spirit in our souls.

Katie Couric says, "Sometimes you are the statue, and sometimes you are the pigeon."

For some people it is uphill both ways. Really bad things really do happen. When they do, we are overwhelmed with the practical need to find the life insurance policy and to ensure that our life goes on, at whatever level it can. Spiritual practices and rituals can help.

We notice how brilliant people are at homemade rituals and homemade language when a tragedy hits. People built altars in the street after 9/11. First flowers; then stuffed animals. A Boston policeman, right after the blast at the marathon, said, "I need all the lanes open here." He meant it. His wise, if exhausted, command goes straight to why we all need to run in the Boston marathon next year, and not in the violence marathon ever. We need all the lanes open, no matter how horrible terrorism becomes. In these mass murders and mass experiences, ritual literally pours out of people. First responders spring into adrenaline-led action. We find ourselves strangely unified in the bonds of community that were quiet before. People give people a glass of water.

CONCLUSION

If none of these rituals move you, make up your own. Remain curious about what is coming next and you will find that you know how to turn crumbs into meaning. Meaning is when we find the inner reality to transform the outer one. Meaning comes when we realize that the way out is the way in. Spirit is usually active if we but notice.

7

REALLY BAD FUNERALS DO HAPPEN

We had the funeral for a famous porn star. The papers all reported it, hundreds of her peers came, and the technology totally messed up. There was a carefully prepared score to go with the slide show, but the carefully prepared score was mistakenly replaced by the tech guy with a lovely sonata by Beethoven. The sonata had been used in morning worship and somehow got in the sleeve of the exciting montage that was to match a professionally prepared video of the deceased person's life. I watched the chief mourner glare at me throughout the entire twenty-minute video. I had no idea what she was glaring about, but I knew something was amiss and I figured it was technical. Everything else was fine. The flowers were in their places. The candles were lit. The montage of photos was appropriately next to the altar. The sanctuary was clean. There were no old sweatshirts hanging around looking for their place in Lost and Found. Bulletins from the morning service had been recycled. The morning's coffee hour had no orphan doughnuts staring out of the garbage can. I found out later that the music had been switched, apologized profusely after remembering a full hour and a half during which I was terrified something irreparable had gone wrong. When the e-mail came two days later, with an extra tip for the tech guy, a nice check for the church, and effusive language talking about how "everything went off without a hitch," I had to have a good long laugh. One technological glitch a mess does not make. In fact, the chief mourner and I had completely different experiences of the same event. She was not glaring at me because of the music. In fact, she didn't even know till later that the music had been a problem. She was just glaring. Her take on the music was, "The Beethoven was lovely and brought out the great grief inside me."

Really bad funerals do happen. They don't happen because there is a technical mistake: there are often technical mistakes. Nor do really bad funerals happen when the wrong color napkins for the collation are chosen. Usually people manage the color of the napkins without even noticing them, no matter how much time was spent deciding which color would be "appropriate."

Sometimes really bad funerals happen because the bereaved are mixed about their grief. One of the emotions you "shouldn't have" is relief. You should be sad, even if you are glad the ordeal is over. Funerals and memorial services can't hold this emotion but a mature person can. Listen to someone describe a typical end of life merry-go-round:

> Sunday was a rough day. He said good-bye to his son and ex-wife and told me he was so tired and wanted to go home to die. So I started making arrangements for hospice care in the hospital with a goal to prepare to bring him home.
>
> Monday morning when I arrived at his room, he was laughing, joking with the nurses and feeling much better. Today the surgeons (I'm so afraid of jinxing it all by talking about it) said they found some live tissue in his heel. That's a good sign, but not a promise. But because he is now eating, watching the Yankees, and reading the newspaper, his own personal care doctor feels he should be in palliative rather than hospice care. Suddenly, he wants to live—says he is prepared to die, but he wants to live.

So . . . where do we go from here? It may be a temporary nursing home, or we may have our hopes up for nothing. I do not want to count my chickens, but the son of a bitch just might lick this! The power of prayer, or just plain stubbornness? Maybe both. I'll say one thing: he'd better start being careful of what he asks for in case someone who loves him gives it to him.

Often by the time the service comes, we have been through the wringer. We have hoped for life, we have hoped for death, we have hoped for a vacation from either, including a vacation from our beloved. So funerals that don't meet their mark can miss because they just can't contain the positive emotions that also surround death. A mourner can speak to her friends about this feeling but rarely in public.

We say, "It's for the best," after the service and before the service and sometimes even during the service. But beware: that "for the best" comment may be heard by those in major projection of their own death as rude and insensitive. Yes, most people attend a funeral as if it is their own. We are rarely able to identify with the other at a time of grief in as mature and full a way as we would like. Funerals and memorial services are crowded with people in serious projection of their own death. Talking about how relieved we are that the ordeal is over can be a mistake in public. Tone of voice matters: try to say, this one, this time, was for the best.

If small or technical mistakes and larger insensitivities regarding relief and grief and their mixture are not the grist for a bad funeral, what is? A bad funeral is one that misses its mark in appropriate grief. Appropriate grief is grief the size of the sadness, no bigger, no smaller. Appropriate grief is also honest. It reads the emotions of those in grief in real time, space, and language as opposed to pretend time and space and language. A child's death is completely different in size and shape from that of a ninety-year-old. A car accident that kills a mother of three is completely different than a car accident that kills a widow. There are degrees to tragedy and the degrees are measured in their consequences to others. I note that people used to wear black to funerals and now only do when the grief is horrific, as in a child's death or a murder. The change in dress is appropriate. Wearing a bright outfit at the funeral of someone who has been murdered is a good example of "bad" in funerals. It is not measuring the size of the grief accurately. It is doing something phony, and phony is the best word for bad I can think of in a funeral.

Other smaller issues can matter. Many people, especially men, get drunk for a funeral. They may act out or act up. They don't ruin the service so much as cause embarrassment to themselves or their friends, partners, and relatives. I had a man show up once for a service, more than a little inebriated, and demand that we sing the "Ave Maria." The embarrassment was all his. It didn't ruin the service. And the organist played the "Ave Maria." There was a wry relaxation afoot as this happened. I had a woman faint while weeping for her husband. She lost control of her sadness. It didn't ruin the service. She experienced a little embarrassment but not much. She was overcome. She was among friends. It didn't matter. In fact, it had such a sense of sincerity that it moved into the realm of the appropriate. It was the right size of her grief.

Many people cry during a service. What I watch for are the people who don't cry. In the clergy folk tradition, we hope for a "three hanky service." That means at least three occasions brought on by music or words or silence where a person can cry and is helped to cry. When a service is so dry that emotions are uninvited, a little bit of bad can happen. The service is designed to bring relief and closure. If that doesn't happen during the service, when will it happen? Tears will come not only at the service or during the ritualized communal ending, but it is helpful if they can come then.

Someone joked that he didn't know what an epiphany was till he had one. That is also true about a good memorial service. Something should happen to us that changes us and completes us and lets us know one time is over and another is beginning. I like to say to people at a wedding or a funeral that you go in as one person and come out as another. If "nothing" happens, the service has failed. If some transition has happened, the service has succeeded.

HOW DO YOU KNOW IF A SERVICE HAS GONE BAD?

As is true with so many things, you won't know if the service failed until you see whether you have transitioned or not. You may not change or become new or healed of your grief because of a bad service. There are hundreds of reasons that can keep you in grief, even in complex grief, the kind that ruins your life the way death took that of your beloved. You can have been wrongly attached to the person in the beginning. We see this in people who are still living with their mothers. When she dies, difficulty in transition is almost guaranteed. There is nothing shameful about this difficulty or about wrongful attachment. These are the facts of life. I'll bet you don't know anyone, including yourself, who is not wrongly attached to something. Right attachment and right connection are ideals. They are rarely realities. Obviously right attachment and right connection, what psychologists call healthy intimacy and spiritual people call right or righteous relationship, prevent bad funerals but that is hardly their primary objective. Good relationships result in good funerals. Difficult relationships result in difficult funerals. If you have read this far in this book, you should not be surprised at this fact.

If you were a sociologist or social psychologist, you could sum up the message of right relationship in three words: constant adaptive change. Relationships take constant tending. They can get better; they can get worse. If you tend them honestly, you will find plenty of solace in a good funeral. It will simply emerge from the right relationship. The opposite is also true.

If you were a biologist, you could say that we live to evolve. If you were a physicist, you would remind your listeners of the way everything is in motion, right down to the smallest particles. You are also in constant motion. You can't stop the wheel of life. It will turn toward death, yours and that of those whom you love. Being practiced at change will help you have the joke and relief of the "best funeral ever."

Let's start with the psychology. At every turn of the wheel, at every stop on the great carousel of life, we are different. We are different physically and biologically as well as psychologically. We remain somewhat the same while turning. Those about to retire are well advised not to move close to where their offspring are living now. Why? Their offspring might move. Those who are planning to have a child will not want to move near their families in hopes of getting childcare: the parents may move or fail or die. Those looking for a partner or life companion may be looking for someone dull this time rather than someone interesting. Those in good health may find that they are not. Those who are in bad health may experience a revival. The fact that your agent sold your last four books doesn't mean she is going to sell this one. The fact that we have always had lots of oil doesn't mean that we will continue to do so. The wheel turns. It keeps turning. The best advice for life at any stage is to never say, "I'll get to that when things settle down." Things don't settle down. They never have and they never will. The wheel turns. There is no way to stop the wheel and stay alive. When death comes, you will probably not be finished. In fact, if there is a good hope and a good way to have a good funeral, it is to make sure that you are not finished at the time of your funeral or that of those whom you love. Those relationships should still be evolving (biologically) and moving (physically.) Each funeral will remind you of all the other losses.

I remember a woman grieving her husband who died suddenly of a heart attack. They were very much in right relationship with each other. They were evolving. They were adapting. They were alive to each other. She was dismayed, though, at the end that all she could think about was the child they lost to illness at age two, some thirty years ago. Grief collects. Grief that is not released or resolved will show up every time you have a funeral. How can you tell what a bad funeral is? It is when a former grief is breathing all the air the current grief should have.

I just lost my associate minister. He has taken a fantastic job, for him, on the West Coast. We have been excellent partners for seven years, give or take a good solid squabble from time to time. I am in funeral mode. I am in motion mode as a chapter is ending. I win the prize for most bereft, by the way. Of course, I thought our ministry here would always be the way it has been. And of course, I also knew that it would not. For now, it is important for me to recognize how normal it is that things don't settle down. We can congratulate ourselves for having had him here for seven years. And I can experience the fact that this loss will remind me of others I've had professionally. I can have a good funeral and just articulate to you or others or anyone who will listen that I am in distress. Permission to be in distress, to be disappointed, to be sad is very important on the road to a good funeral. Absent that permission, you are on your way to a bad one.

Ezekiel's great wheel comes to mind. Check it out in the first chapter of the Bible book by his name. It is a wild and crazy vision of wheels within wheels within wheels. And that is where we are when we are in active grief. We are remembering the last associate we lost or the child we lost as well as experiencing the new wound. When we become people who join Ezekiel in seeing the wheel, way up in the middle of the air, we don't have to like the wheel we see. We can still hope for things to concretize, settle down, stop whirling. But we will find ourselves soon in the search for a more satisfying hope. We can hate the change we see or dislike it fiercely. We don't have to like the wheel to see the wheel. But we are helped by knowing that everything is in constant motion, including ourselves.

I was at a delightful retreat center near Santa Barbara once. The man at the desk had a twinkle in his eye most of the time. He said that every day all day long, people came into the registration center and asked to be directed to the labyrinth so they could walk it. He learned to respond as follows: if you are still looking for the labyrinth that means you are already in it. Yup. Asking for the location of the labyrinth is a really dumb question. Or as our retreat leader said, Let's get rid of that question. "Finished." I am now finished, we say, when our hopes for ourselves march straight into the labyrinth of constant change. He suggested that we replace the word "finished" with the word "refinished." That we imagine ourselves deepening into personal luster by constant polishing. By constant threshing by the millstone of life. I like the idea of being refinished. I don't like the idea of being finished. A bad funeral imagines it can finish things. It can't. It just thrusts us into another turn of the wheel.

Or consider the bicycle, another kind of labyrinth, another kind of wheel. Riding a bike is something that once you know how to do, you don't forget. When you approach a funeral with your heart full of former griefs, it is important to accept their presence. You don't have to grieve your mother when you are burying your husband. But she can also be there. Like riding a bicycle, grieving is something you don't forget how to do. In fact, every time you have a grief, you get better at it. Grief, like biking, is also a balance and power issue, both at the same time. Power often says things are going to settle down. Balance often says the opposite, keep pumping. You'll get somewhere.

My friend Pat De Jong once preached a sermon at First Church Berkeley in which she said that she and her husband had just finished a bike trip through Europe. They biked thirty-two miles a day. The first night they were so tired that they fell asleep with their helmets on their heads. When they woke up in the morning, face down on their pillows, helmets on, they laughed and laughed. They had made it through their first day, with nothing more serious than fatigue. When you see the wheel, you don't fear fatigue or injury so much. You understand that you are turning and that you may as well peek around the next corner. People who are finished try to stop the wheel from turning. People who are biking the labyrinth of life are always building a better yesterday. People who can embrace motion understand that every saint has a past, every sinner a future. When we wheel through life, we feel the fear and turn the wheel anyway. We know the exhaustion of death and dying and often go to sleep with our helmets on. Better put, the wheels on the bus go round and round. Or as Ezekiel concludes the first part of his vision, there are wheels within wheels within wheels. A bad funeral tries to wrap things up and finish them. A bad funeral thinks it should be something other than what it is. A good funeral wheels into the wheels of life.

The best advice I ever got about a terrible personal grief was from a woman I only sort of know. She was fifty-nine then; I was twenty-eight. I had divorced my husband, whom I had married at nineteen. I really thought I was lost and finished. I asked her if it would ever be "over," this pain, this constant pain. She said, "Yes, one morning you will wake up and it will just be over. You won't know when. You won't know how. You'll just know that the pain is gone and that you are back on the main road of your life." She was right. The wheels keep turning.

MEMORIALS

Let's apply the personal wisdom about wheeling—what I might even call freewheeling through the funeral—to the business of the word "memorial" itself. We have been using the funeral and the memorial service language interchangeably. We also know that the memorial service is intended to remember something. Its intent is actually to remember well or appropriately. Likewise the physical memorials of our worlds. Sometimes they help us remember well and sometimes they don't. The question of a good funeral or a bad one is also answered by which physical memorials work and which don't. They go back to the question of honest and rightsized memory.

I think first of the memorial at Ground Zero. Now thousands of people throng there daily, looking at the cascading pools, taking selfies, looking at pictures of crushed emergency trucks. The memorial had been highly contested architecturally in New York City, but it is now up. Freedom Tower is enormous, beautiful, singular, and ironically, the most highly secure place in the city. Does a memorial to freedom work when terrorism causes security measures to be so enormous? Is the memorial an honest one?

New Yorker critic Adam Gopnik has argued that it is not a living or useful memorial because its truths are so paradoxical, full of security after terror. And security measures can't really stop terror, as we have learned at Sandy Hook Elementary. Memorial services work if they are honest, even honest about helplessness.

A funeral service can "work" even if the person being buried is one whom many are happy to bury. But that paradox has to prevail and find some expression. Because paradox is part of so many of our lives, if not most of our lives, it is important to fear the grandiose or the perplexing in the funeral. Simpler is always better. Ellis Island is a great memorial because people can participate in it and at it. It is small enough to have a million doors and entry points. Ground Zero may have just become too big—in the same way that the terror of 9/11 was too big for us to manage. Gopnik argues that "the greatest of modern American memorials is Maya Lin's 1982 design for the Vietnam Veterans Memorial, in Washington. She made it local and indigenous instead of grand and fixed." Again, this is helpful information. People started bringing mementoes of their lost loved ones to the monument. Some even brought bottles of Jack Daniels and deposited them in front of their friend's name. At first the park police said no. Then they said yes, allowing people to participate. For me, the most heart-wrenching three-hankie experience around 9/11 was all the stuffed animals, thoroughly wet and absurd, that stayed for days and days after the mass murder.

Or consider the Oklahoma City tragedy. In the end, a simple field of empty chairs was created, one named for each of the victims, with smaller chairs for the children killed. Such simplicity is elegant. It also rightsizes the grief, allowing the large grief a small setting in which to make real and realize itself.

When it comes to 9/11 and its memorials, the most moving architectural memorial is the "Project for the Immediate Reconstruction of Manhattan's Skyline" (as it was then named), which appeared a mere six months after the disaster. Eighty-some searchlights rise at night from the ground to space itself, or so it seems, forming two columns of lights where the towers had once been, imitating their twinning and rising out of their destruction. That light replacing concrete and steel is amazing. Ashes to ashes became stardust to stardust. I remember seeing them one night from my office, a mile north. I cried and cried and cried some more. There was nothing else to do. A bad funeral doesn't elicit tears. A good funeral does elicit tears, the kind that make your belly hurt. Sometimes the formal funeral or memorial service will find its rival in an informal one.

Once I got talked into spreading the ashes of an elderly man on the sidewalk where he lived. The Department of Health would not have been happy. But neither do they know. There was relief then that the service had not provided. Once I convinced emergency room staff at a Miami hospital to let me see the body of my associate minister. Yes, I know what you are thinking. He had died of a heart attack at his apartment in Northside. The ambulance wouldn't wait for us to get through the traffic. We bribed the ambulance driver, whom we met at the hospital. We unzipped the bag and had a little service in the parking lot. Another time I needed to say good-bye to someone very dear to me. His wife was in the way, as she should be. I talked the nurse into letting me say prayers in the morgue with a couple of friends of mine. Again, a good memorial is rightsized. It may even have a little stealth to it.

What can we learn about memorials from architecturally dead memorials and living ones? We can learn that we have to participate in them very simply in order for them to be good for us. The unbidden bicycle is an unridden bicycle. Having Harry's Glittermobile leave the sanctuary and hit the streets was a very good example of an informal memorial service. We can innovate a good memorial service even if the official one doesn't take or is emotionally dishonest or just wrong. And even if the official one does result in change and transition, there is no reason not to continue to ritually mourn "outside" or in informal ways.

Finally, if cycling doesn't strike you as a good guide to the ongoing nature of a memorial service, or the memorial business doesn't work for you, consider a biological one. Beth Shapiro is a scientist who is working on de-extinction. Yup. De-extinction. She brings species back from the dead. She tells us a lot about adaptive change and how constant adaptive change is the way to survive. She worries about bringing back animals that were extinct because they won't help the wheel. She says that she is much more interested in de-extinction so that we can find out how some species survive climate change, which they have. For her, evolution is God. She is not concerned about any one species so much as about habitat. In the same way, as a gardener I care about soil, not flowers, and as a minister, I care about process, not product. In matters of habitat and soil and process, we find wheels that can turn. With biology and evolution, we get rid of species that gum up the wheels. Or at least withdraw their oxygen. Thus the only question here is how the memorial remains unfinished. How we never let it stop turning.

Let's say your beloved died ten years ago and you haven't stopped grieving. You need help. You need another memorial service. You might have it on the anniversary of his or her death. Or on their birthday. Or on your anniversary, if you were married. Have one. Try again. The wheel keeps turning.

There are wheels within wheels within wheels. We ride them as a way of life, a way of living, and a way of living for hope to result from our memories.

ACCIDENTAL FUNERALS MAY HAPPEN BEFORE YOU ARE READY

It is never too early to have a good funeral. Especially if you don't trust your posse or tribe to bury you well, you may want to be alert for a good experience of a good funeral for yourself before the end.

We had sailed at dusk on Biscayne Bay. We were out for about four hours when our captain turned toward home. Usually, in other sails, she had turned on the engine as we approached the dock. Her boat, a sailing instructor's boat, is docked at the far end of the marina in a corner, a bit of a tight squeeze but not impossible with the engine going. This night she got a twinkle in her eye as we turned toward home. "Let's try it without the engine. I think the conditions are right." Minutes later she added, "We may have to turn the engine on at the last minute so be ready . . . we won't know till we get close." Moments later we glided, soundlessly and effortlessly and enginelessly, into the berth.

There was a calm in that moment that deserves respect and attention. It was quieter than I have ever heard. I used to think you couldn't hear quiet. Now I know you can. It was less effort than I have experienced in a long time. Effort is a persistent intruder in my life: even getting to this sail had required it. I didn't know if I had time, didn't know if it would be enough fun to warrant the time off and away, wondered if I had brought the right dish for my part of the potluck, blah blah blah. Enginelessness, however, was an utterly new experience. Enginelessness is on the other side of effortlessness: it is not the absence of struggle so much as the presence of peace. I want more life with the engine off. I want its quiet most of all. On this night I experienced what I want in my funeral.

I want to be effortlessly quiet. And I daresay that is a goal that I can achieve.

In "Small Silences: Listening for the Lessons of Nature," an essay in the July 2004 issue of *Harper's*, Edward Hoagland (a nature writer and lion tamer) says, "It is hard to even find a sight line without buildings, pavement, people . . . and we're not even awed by each other anymore. Even people are too much of a good thing" (52). I long for quiet and have longed for quiet for a long time. Experiencing that quiet was an "achievement" for me.

As a biologist, Hoagland thinks that God created the world for the bubbles. For the froth. In other words, God wasn't using engines functionally, to get from one place to the other. God was developing engines for their fun and froth, their evidence of the magnificence of creation. Perhaps abundance is frothy instead of functional. In other words, one sail like this particular night's sail is plenty. Having to work harder to get a bigger and better boat is too much. There is a difference between abundance and too much, and way too many of us know it. We know the difference between abundance and saturation. Hoagland says, "Glee is like the froth on a beer or on cocoa. Not essential. Glee is effervescence. It is bubbles in the water, beyond efficiency, which your thirst doesn't actually need." Hoagland doesn't have much to say about God, only this: "The thread in God's creation is . . . ebullience. . . . The choosiest females choose not just for strength or money, but also for the superfluous energy that humor and panache imply." Hoagland reveres evolution more than most people revere God. And evolution is quiet and slow. You can't even really tell that it is happening or that you are participating in it. But because you and your genome and habitat are participating in evolution, it is appropriate to know its quiet.

The peace of enginelessness is also frothy. It moves beyond the world of evolution and utility and gotta gotta gotta. Enginelessness is not useful at all. But without its peace, life is just bread, just "gotta eat," just biological, just repetitive effort on behalf of the species in us and after us. Some people have figured out the way to engineless abundance. I think of the Italians who speak of the "sistemati" or settled way of the evening stroll (the *passeggiata*), or the *bella figura*. They swear that change only comes so that things may stay the same. They find purpose for life in the pursuit of beauty. Beauty is the saving grace of evolution. Beauty saves the grace in evolution. Another key to enginelessness is to find peace in beauty. We know that Bach's concerti were beautiful because of what he left out as well as what he put in. Even hot chocolate can have too much froth—and spill and stain and make a mess of what otherwise might be purely delicious. Interior decorators join the accumulated wisdom about the engine. "Fewer finer" is what every decorator will tell you. Gardeners too. Pruning a bush makes it grow beautifully. Letting it overtake your yard has nothing to do with beauty.

Turning off the engine is a good idea if we want peace or beauty or quiet in our life. You don't have to be a poet to understand this meaning. You don't have to out-Bach Bach. You can be an ordinary person living an ordinary life. I went to the store to buy a new pair of blue jeans. The clerk asked if I wanted slim fit, easy fit, or relaxed fit, regular or faded, stonewashed or acid washed, button fly or regular fly . . . and that's when I started to sputter. Can't I just have a pair of blue jeans, size 14? I feel the same way about my funeral: there is an elegance in a simple service. We can overthink a funeral just the way we can overthink just about anything.

CONCLUSION

Turning off our engines gives us a capacity for quiet. We achieve wellness in quiet ways, even at end times. The best funeral is the most effortless one. The worst funeral is the one that is overdone, overthought, made up by overfunctioning people who imagine that more functioning will assuage the matter of death and dying. It won't.

Wellness is a final confidence in solitude. It is a good way to live: engines are important some of the time but not all of the time. Jesus did come so that we might have life and have it more abundantly. Turning off our engines and sailing quietly all the way home is also good practice for dying. We glide into our next berth, ready, grateful, and without a lot of noise in the background. Really bad funerals happen when there is too much background and not enough ground, too much noise and not enough quiet, too much worry and not enough confidence.

8

FINDING A SPIRITUAL HOME
BEFORE DEATH

People say over and over again that they want to die at home. What does that mean? Where the hell is home? Especially when most of us move around a lot and find that we have to carry our tents within us.

In this chapter I argue that a spiritual home is the best and only place from which a good death can emerge. Dying homeless is too tragic, unnecessary, and sad. What is a spiritual home? It is a place where your spirit takes off its shoes, sits on its couch, and leaves its life, accompanied by music, beauty, and choice. For some it is a congregation. For others it is anything but that. This chapter helps you see what a congregation can give you, before you die, and makes an unapologetic argument for belonging. Why? Because most of us don't sense that we belong and it hurts and harms us and those we love.

After I make the strongest possible argument I can for a community here on earth, as a way to prepare for the best funeral ever, I will allow that some people just need to be by themselves. I remember Ed. Members of his congregation always brought him flowers at the nursing home where he died. "I don't like flowers." They visited him with regularity. "I don't like visitors."

What did Ed like? He liked to go on cruises and ask for a table for one. That preference became the theme of his funeral after he died. His ashes were scattered (extralegally in the San Francisco Bay by a hired boat captain who knew exactly how to jimmy the system), and as they flew, they were seen gray against the gray fog. And that's when the Princess Cruise ship emerged out of the cloudiness. Ed had ordered it, some said. Ed didn't want a spiritual home and got one anyway. Eight people were on the rented boat that day to say good-bye to this popular loner. One hundred fifty people attended his funeral. Ed was gruff enough to be liked. He was unique enough to be loved. Maybe the spiritual home that Ed found didn't matter to him. But it did matter to those who became fond of him and scattered flowers into the bay alongside his ashes. Sometimes the spiritual home we don't have ourselves can come around us in those who care for us. Why would we curse the ones who follow us by not giving them the home they wanted in us? In other words, a spiritual home is a comfort at the end. You may not want one. But those who follow you will want one for you.

Obviously, and to repeat, you may not think you need a spiritual home. You may think that friends and family are enough. If so, at least read through this chapter with an open heart and mind. You may be depriving friends and family of something they can use as well, especially after you are gone. My father-in-law often said the best decision he ever made was to join an assisted living group early enough to establish himself among his peers. Now that he is in late dotage, having just broken a hip at ninety years, he is surrounded by friends and family and community. A spiritual home doesn't have to be a congregation, although congregations excel at death and dying. A spiritual home can instead be a group of peers, of people who know us, a group where you are welcome and known.

So here come the arguments for finding a spiritual home for yourself, and if not for yourself, then for others.

ARGUMENTS FOR FINDING A SPIRITUAL HOME

Argument One

Why "darken the door" of a spiritual place only on the day of your death? Why be a stranger on your way to a new kind of home? Annual ritual observance, even Christmas and Easter or Yom Kippur or Rosh Hashanah, allows you the kind of preparation you need. At least you know where to park. At least you know something about where others will park when they bid farewell to you. Having a spiritual home is a lot like personal maintenance or spiritual preparation. It is the opposite of "delayed maintenance," which of course is the most expensive kind of all.

Spirited people pay attention to their fishing lines and maintain their boats. They tie good knots and hang good hooks. Then they go fishing. Sam Kestenbaum, a lobsterman in Maine, wrote of observing Yom Kippur at sea in the *New York Times*, September 14, 2010: "It wasn't boat work but it was work—a kind of repair, a checking of the knots and wiring, refueling for another year."

You can't get much more ordinary than by going to work on a boat. But there, in the ordinary, you find the extraordinary. There with the help of an annual religious observance, you can be reminded of what your soul needs. Religious institutions guard religious observances. They can be useful in finding a spiritual home. You don't have to obey all their rules to reap their benefit. You can fish for lobster and still be a Jew, one attentive to his lines. But you don't have to move into the cul-de-sac of nonengagement with your past, people, or future. You don't have to be a stranger to a congregation when you begin to look for a place from which to leave earth.

Of course you can use a funeral parlor or a forest as well. You don't need to depart from a sacred site. Spiritual preparation for death involves having a place that you call a spiritual home from which you will exit. A funeral parlor can suffice but it cannot enrich. It turns the departure into something functional as opposed to something beautiful. If your theology of death is functional, as in you need to rent a parlor from which to exit, then by all means, use one. But if your theology of death is transcendent and reaching for meaning, think about joining all the people who maintain their lines in ritual observances year-round. You will find it helpful to be with nonexperts who are trying to become experts.

Argument Two

Spiritual populists are wary of "protective self-marginalization," a great concept of a theologian named Hal Taussig. It means fearing vulnerability so much that you extend its fear to institutions. It means protecting yourself before you get hurt in such a way that you refuse many benefits along the way. You are different. You are special. You don't need what other people need. From here you can get very, very lonely—but at least you won't get hurt. Protective self-marginalization results in a cul-de-sac. Religious institutions don't have meaning because we don't try their meanings on for size.

Many say they don't like the taste of "organized religion." If they only knew how disorganized religion really is, they wouldn't dare that critique. You can find an organized or disorganized community of faith in which to be comforted, challenged, and connected. The food, the house, and the people will be both imperfect and nourishing. Think "lived in." Your spiritual home might not be a "regular" congregation. Instead it might be a place aside, a habit habituated, a Tuesday night reading group, a prayer group, or a "consciousness raising" breakfast—an energy exchange on the edge of an established congregation. Think "house church." A group of Koreans meets every Sunday afternoon in my congregation's building. They pray and sing in their own language. That is a great model for "organized religion" if you just can't stand or find something established. Either way, your religious home will involve others, many of whom are as clumsy as you are as a spiritual person. If you set out to find a perfect religious institution in which to die, you will get hurt and you will be disappointed. If you set out to find an imperfect one, you will be surprisingly pleased.

Argument Three

Remaining lackadaisical about your spiritual home is unwise. Name and own that you want a little comfort, a little challenge, and a lot of connection. Why not ask for what you want? Repeat: Don't be a perfectionist about it. Instead demand it of yourself and others. If you need to, create it. Don't let all the good real estate at the center of town go to a spiritual place that bores you or makes you feel dishonest by overblown claims. Find a synagogue or a mosque or a church that is genuine. Use it. Or find a phony one, or one that is not yet realized. Change it. Get over the boredom and hypocrisy that many of us knew as children, and move forward into a world that frees and shapes our spirits. Once you become a part of a religious congregation, you get the opportunity to make it what it is. You get to participate. You raise its standards to those of your own for the people of God. Who else will do it for you?

Even you could find a spiritual home that didn't embarrass you, dumb you down, make you tell spiritual lies, or just plain bore you. You could find a spiritual home that gave the rest of your life meaning, joy, and purpose—and refused to demean or dichotomize the suffering you also knew. You could find a home that was not punishmentalist toward gays or immigrants or Muslims or other "others." You could be both a guest and a host in that home, one who serves and is served. You might even shiver with some grace or know some salvation, if and as you enter the spiritual world of religion as an adult. What is salvation? Its root words are safety, sanctuary, shalom, security in a community, sheltered by God. Don't you want to be safe at the end? Especially since you know how dangerous the crossing is.

Argument 4

A spiritual adult removes the rose-colored glasses and looks anew at what is real in religion and spirituality. The religious words do need liberation from religion! Who will do that if not us? Who owns religion, if not us? Who is in charge of your spirituality, if not you? Growing up means abandoning the notion that someone else is in charge besides you. And if you are lucky, you will die as an adult, not as a child.

Argument 5

Beware of vanilla or generalized spirituality. Know what you mean if you find yourself saying, "I am spiritual but not religious." It also is a cul-de-sac, a dead end, a place from which it is hard to "be buried." Many of the Nones (none of the above) have a lot of everything going on. They are not "none." They are "some of the above." Why not be a some-of-the-above kind of person with a minimalist spiritual home? Even if you have to make it yourself.

The first step out of the cul-de-sac of the cliché that we are "spiritual but not religious" has to do with a little tenderness toward others and ourselves. Get over embarrassment at your use of clichés! We're all in this century together. The tenderness involves testing, testing, and testing some more. We test the meaning of our own words: how can you be spiritual but not religious? What is that self-description doing for us? We take a turn out of our cul-de-sac. We might go to church on a Sunday and just listen. We observe. We respect. We attend synagogue on a Friday night and just listen, observe, and respect. If we send our children to Hebrew school, and know that third graders just can't learn another language at 3 in the afternoon on Tuesdays, we change the method of initiating children to Judaism. We become spiritual activists, those who claim a place at the table after sitting with others who want what we want. Yes, this spiritual activism is as hard as changing the school lunch program. It involves a turn out from where we have been, a different route, one which acknowledges that what we are doing now isn't doing all for us, spiritually, that it could. I am not arguing that any of this is easy, only that its difficulty is easier than the daily dismal of accepting things as they are and leaving your child—or the spiritual child within you—uninitiated to a spiritual and religious tribe. Finding a spiritual home is the decision to die within a tribe, not outside one.

You may not want to have to work at your spirituality. But then again you may also not want to be bereft or have to hire an institution to marry, bury, or baptize you and yours. You might want an organic relationship with the places where you have your rights of passage and initiation. You may decide to go back to the religion of your birth or to move on to something new and different. You might want to belong. If you want to belong—and to be authentic and honest in that belonging—you are going to have to work at it. The work might even be fun. But it won't be fun for a while. It will take some time.

AFTER THE ARGUMENTS

There will be many obstacles in the way of your finding a spiritual home. Even if you accept all five of the arguments, you will only be at the beginning of the road to your spiritual home. There will be many obstacles along the way. You should be spiritually prepared for disappointment—and powerfully convinced that you want to die with a people and a place anyway.

Most congregations today are desperate for new people—and then reject them or put them through absurd initiation rites on the way in. If you want a spiritual home, you may have to make one. That means testing a home and then renovating a home. Lots of people like building and designing their own homes; it can be fun. Even after you build and design your own home, you will have to sustain it, keep it "up." It will never be done if it is a place worth living in. In my forty years of ordained ministry, I have watched "newcomers" claw their way into the old ways. My congregations have consistently turned around from the old-timer ownership of the institution to the seekers owning it. I tell people not to come just once for worship but to come at least six months—and a good Easter or Christmas—before they begin to enjoy the sound of the organ or the language of the prayers. To find a spiritual home, populists need to test, test, and test some more; shop, shop, and shop some more; sit, sit, and sit some more. We get to take the jeans back to the store only after we have worked them "in."

It is likely that your spiritual home is close by and ordinary. You probably don't need to go to Tibet to find a spiritual experience. Often we exoticize what it might mean to have a spiritual home when, even without a first-class seat on a jet to the East, we are touched by a neighbor who knows where there is a good choir, who sometimes lifts her heart of a Sunday. Ask around your office or your neighborhood or your gym. Somebody may have just the right imperfect community of people for your imperfections as a person.

I often say to people, "Try three congregations before you even think about committing to one." Then, when you do find one you sort of like, visit it for six months. Every Sunday is not magnificent in every parish. Speaking as a preacher, I must confess I have three or four good sermons a year. The rest are satisfactory but not mind or heart boggling. If, after an openhearted look and some serious testing, let's say three or six months each, if then you still don't feel at home anywhere, create a prayer group or a spiritual consciousness-raising group. Meet on Saturday mornings over coffee. Talk about what matters to you. Speak of your longings. Be vulnerable with people. Your search is for grace and salvation—not an institution. Finding the Spirit is essential; a home—or bucket—for them is important, but neither urgent nor essential. When I advocate institutional companionship in your tango, I don't have any one bucket in mind. Instead I have in mind SOME bucket. You need a group, a place, a process. That group can become your congregation, your sacred space, your ritual. If you can't find a bucket, after serious testing of three or so, then create one. Don't try to live without a spiritual bucket: that is my hope for the spiritually hungry. Why stay hungry when you could eat? Why not be a populist with the power you do have to ask the Spirit to dance?

How do you know if you have found a good spiritual home for you? You will know by whether or not you are deepening and ripening. The criteria for a spiritual home is your spiritual development. Are you growing there? Are you finding yourself more comforted, challenged, connected? If yes, good. If not, move on. But move on only after you have gotten over the small stuff. You are looking for a place from which to die. It will not be perfect. Instead it will be "lived in."

A lot of us use a lot of excuses to avoid spiritual homes. "They" don't worship right or talk too much about money, or sing badly. Maybe they do. That doesn't mean that you can't find meaning there. Or make meaning there.

A spiritual home helps us understand what Martin Luther meant by "adiaphora." Adiaphora are that which are not essential. Which involves most things. You have a better shot at the essentials if you also pay attention to the nonessentials, like getting yourself into an environment where your spirituality can flourish. You may find grace in Tibet or in a weekly walk in the forest. Mazel tov. You also might be more able to sustain that experience of grace in a community, one that knows reverses and shifting gears. The best thing about belonging to a congregation is that someone shows up at the hospital to visit you or your kid, that hospital which wasn't on your horizon the day before.

You will learn very quickly what is not essential after you break your hip and "just want to get back to yesterday." In the twinkle of an eye, you can find yourself facing permanent disability, even death. You will have to find courage that you know you don't have. You will need help. Religious organizations know how to help. All parts of them may not know how to help but enough will to make them your friend the day after your hip is broken.

Hopefully, you will have tested the religious institution of your choice long before you break your hip. Or begin to meet your maker. A spiritual home is not just a people and a place. It is also a text, a big story into which we fit our lives. You will want to test the texts before you will fully belong.

Texts—the Bible, the Koran, and the Torah—are the best part of religious institutions. I suggest NOT reading a sacred text all the way through so much as using an ancient way of hearing the scriptures. Most people don't know that every three years Christian congregations read their way through the readable parts of the Bible in service. In Jewish congregations a similar "lectionary" is used. Lectio Divina is also an ancient practice where people read a small portion of the readable parts every day. Very few people know that scriptures are 80 percent unreadable. That may be a metaphor for the entire religious experience. Twenty percent of the texts will take you over the top in inspiration. You will wonder how those ancient people could have known that "there is a river whose streams make glad the city of God" (Psalm 46). The other 80 percent will mystify you or make you feel stupid. Indeed, why are there so many wars in the Bible, so much violence, so much adultery, so much shame about making money or being successful? Religious texts are not perfect. Nor are they the "divine and unchanging word of God." God is still speaking. One of the biggest secrets of spirituality is that it is something by and for people. It is human made, including the ancient texts. Even they are populist, born in one time and place, constantly renovating their kitchens. You CAN'T read them from beginning to end. I watch people try and I watch them fail. Instead, we might consider the lection—the readings as chosen by other human beings over centuries. Attending a worship service for a series of months and seasons and being willing to be bored will set you on the path of spirituality. It will be populist because it will be tender toward the human in you and the human in others. Even if you come to religious life and spiritual home "too late," there is still plenty of time to read the texts, no matter how disabled you are. You can even have them read to you. You can enter the joy and gladness of midrash. You are not the first person to have died. You are not the last either. Midrash will place you in an honest place in your time and culture. Why not use it?

IF YOU FAIL TO FIND A SPIRITUAL HOME

Still another way to find a populist spiritual home is to simply meditate. When we meditate, we sift the intensity of our experience into the important and the less important. As we meditate, congregate, and pray, we will want to engage a bit of spiritual therapy and look at how much of our spiritual loneliness is our own "fault." I don't believe in the word *fault* so this will be tricky. Instead I will gently ask how much of you is really resisting being at home spiritually. You may not be at fault but you may be responsible, which is to say, you are in charge. There are logs you can remove from your eyes so that you can begin to see.

Meditation helps us see. It does so by stopping the clock from performance anxiety. It can also absorb the awful defeat of not being able to find a people or a place or a meaningful story into which to textualize our lives. Meditation turns us inward long enough to remember who we are, what we want, where we are going. That is what is called a spiritual home: the center of knowing who we are, what we want, where we are going. A good question for meditation is "If I had all the resources I needed, who would I be?" Another good question for meditation is "If I decided not to follow my cultural marching orders, even for a day, who would I be?" Some of us find we have to ask these questions over and over, as their answers change and so do we.

While congregating, praying, or meditating, even singing the Sacred into our daily lives, we will discover we must be spiritual entrepreneurs. There is nothing dumb about the resistance of so many of us to organized religion. There is nothing wrong with you if you can't find a religious and spiritual home. We have all been to the dowdy digs. We have seen the old-timers tell the seekers that they don't really belong, as if the old-timers didn't inherit the sacred space, as if it was their own personal property. We have watched the punishmentalists take over religion and declare it a matter of morality or do-goodism, as though Jesus and the rest didn't tell us that self-righteousness was the one sin God might not be able to forgive. Spiritual entrepreneurs make a way where there is no way. We innovate and initiate—and put up with rudeness—so urgent are we to get home.

Meditation as a spiritual practice can be a kind of home. It can take the brunt off the loss of being spiritually homeless, especially late in life.

If meditation is something that puts you to sleep or bores you, find a walking or action meditation. Swim yourself to peace. Or take naps while trying to meditate. Walking meditation is a very helpful way to stay on the trail and to find a trail. Many who have been disappointed by organized religion are not disappointed by nature.

You will want to develop some very small personal rituals. Mine is stick gathering at my little country place sixty miles north of Manhattan. We have an outdoor fireplace. My best idea for a walking prayer is to hit the Appalachian Trail, outside my door, and to return with a handful of sticks. These light a fire at night. I don't really know why I pick up sticks and burn them. I do know that I calm into a sense of light and fire and ritual when I do this. I know that when I am disabled and at death's door, I will remember the sticks and the walks and the white blazes on the trail.

I know many others have "little" practices that warm them. Many like to practice for death. They like to be involved with death in the congregation. Some make a casserole and deliver it the second they find out someone has faced bad news. When my parishioners hear that someone has died or received news of the death of a child, they get out their casserole dishes. The casserole doesn't get close to consoling the death. It only tries. When you are part of a spiritual home, people stand by you and you stand by them. Many who suffer will tell you their refrigerator became absurdly full. Why? People want to "do something" when faced with the absurdity.

The portability of our spiritual home may be important. Death won't necessarily come when we are at home! Instead a spiritual home is a kind of energy exchange, like the lighting of a fire, or a ritual that makes the heavy light or the empty full. A casserole may be an absurd response to a parent whose child was hit by a car. But it is what we have.

CONCLUSION: IT SEEMS TO ME THAT THIS ONE IS GOOD ENOUGH

Often, when we find our spiritual home, we usually tell the story of how it found us. We did the entire match questing, signed up on all the sites, kept ourselves "up," and then showed up at the right place at the right time and shivered with a little gladness. We were also scared stiff. We wanted to be accepted with all the joy of our own acceptance of the other. We were so afraid that might not happen. When it did happen, we were overjoyed. In a spiritual home that gladness becomes the experience of grace. What is grace? Unexpected, surprising, unmerited gladness.

When we experience grace through a spiritual home, we find we are OK just the way we are, where we are, how we are. Your litmus test for a spiritual home is whether your troubles and your triumphs, your gifts and your weaknesses are used and recognized and affirmed there. All of you come through the door of a spiritual home, not just the polished parts. When you get the shoulds and the resume out of the way, the door just opens up. As the Boston policeman said, "We need all the lanes open here." In a spiritual home, the lanes from life to death are open and accompanied for you and for those you will be privileged to die with.

It is interesting how religion gave over death to funeral directors, hospice, and hospital beds. This outsourcing comes straight from the refusal to go deeper than "I'm spiritual but not religious." And because of that refusal, now, even the experience of death and dying can be bought and sold. Finding and maintaining a spiritual home can be the most revolutionary thing you can do.

If revolution is not of interest to you, imagine this: you too can change and be the person you want to be.

9

MY LORD, WHAT A MORNING

If you don't know that old hymn "My Lord What a Morning," check it out. It is a Black spiritual, written in the United States during the eighteenth or nineteenth century. Joan Baez and many other artists have recorded it. It is another version of eternity, a sense of the end time at the end of time. It speaks of stars falling in another kind of morning, a new day that has come which wakes up all the nations underground. As a Christian, the point of my life has been to be a part of God's time. It has been to participate in the "already but not yet" of God's time, referred to formerly as bringing in the kingdom of God or the commonwealth of God or the time of God. We say that eschatology—what happens at the end—is the redemption of creation—what happened at the beginning. Between alpha and omega, we live in the promise of the good time and we help to bring it along. We are gifted both by the coming time of God and the agents within it. That is a lot of language to describe what it means to say, "My Lord, What a Morning." More simply, we can't wait for the end time because then all will be well, all will eat, all will be treated fairly, and all will have a song in their heart. When I pray in public, over a meal, I often simply say, "Will all who are grateful please raise their right hand?" Or "Hasten the day, O God, when everyone will eat as well as we will tonight."

The song gives one version—a Christian one—of the end of time. As a Christian plus, and not just a Christian, I think of it as one way to think about the end of time. I am content with "just" metaphors. I love my metaphor renewal programs. I also love the song because my picture of my own death is "ashes to ashes, stardust to stardust," as stated repeatedly in the previous chapters. I don't think that the end time for me is the end time for everything. It is just the end time for me. Thus, in the singing of this song, I remember the future that is coming. When all time is transformed into good time for all people, the stars will be so surprised they will probably fall.

These are the words:

> My Lord, what a morning!
> My Lord, what a morning!
> Oh, my Lord, what a morning
> when the stars begin to fall.
> Oh, you will hear the trumpet sound
> to wake the nations underground,
> Looking to my Lord's right hand
> when the stars begin to fall.
> Oh, you will see my Jesus come,
> His glory shining like the sun,
> Looking to my Lord's right hand
> When the stars begin to fall.
> Oh, you will hear all Christians shout,
> 'Cause there's a new day come about,
> Looking to my Lord's right hand
> When the stars begin to fall.
> My Lord, what a morning!
> My Lord, what a morning!
> Oh, my Lord, what a morning
> when the stars begin to fall.

I want this hymn sung at my funeral because it gives me great hope. I also want the "Itsy Bitsy Spider." but that is another matter entirely. I hope that my speckness will have been part of a great project, the project of God's time. I hope to have played a small role in a large drama. As we end this book, it will be important to think about what comes next. It will be important not to confuse our end with the end. That being said, there is nothing unimportant about our end or our life. Instead, it fits into a larger framework and larger package, which is the stardust and the coming twinkling time of God.

Here I will summarize the themes of the previous chapters into what you can expect the morning after you die or the morning after your loved one dies. I will go back through the spiritual practices of midrash and blessing, of enginelessness and having the talk. The talk requires you to be an engine. When you are sure you've had it enough times, you can release your grip on the throttle.

This book has been about both you and those close to you. It has been about how you prepare for the inevitable for yourself or others. We have looked at sample services for a variety of kinds of people. We have talked about the time when you might be sick before you die and talked about ways to use sickness as a rehearsal for dying. We have talked about the spiritual and practical checklist, which hopefully you will have completed before death comes to you or yours. If all the work in early dotage was impossible to complete—and yes, it is work—then you will have one kind of grief. It will be mourning and grief plus a lot of practical details that may come close to being overwhelming.

If you are lucky enough to have had time to prepare practically for the "getting your affairs in order" stage of living, then you will have a simpler mourning. You will be able to attend to what you are feeling. You will know gratitude and grief on a first name basis; there won't be a layer of paperwork between you and them.

There will still be extraordinary amounts of "stuff" to do—like remembering to get at least fifty death certificates from the doctor because you will need them—but you will not be the victim of detail mania getting in the way of grief. When detail mania takes over at the time of death, the delay in genuine feeling of genuine loss can be very dangerous. You may also forget the depth of gratitude you know in living. People can still constantly question whether they are doing it "right," which of course is the wrong question, even when friendly with gratitude and grief in varying proportions. But if your mind is not your own and your heart is distracted, the wrong questions will surely be on your table.

I will write this final chapter as though you have done the work—and as though you have not. There is no "should" or "judgy" here. Sometimes we are lucky enough to prepare for death and sometimes we are not.

THE MORNING AFTER YOU DIE

You will not know where you are, unless we are dead wrong about immortality. I have been arguing that we don't know, can't know, and won't know. We may not even know if our soul is alive and our body gone and that we are in line for a recycling with all the others who died yesterday. Death is surely the loss of the consciousness we knew and the breath we had. Beyond that, there is little that can be said.

That little being said, you can imagine that your lost consciousness is being profoundly experienced by those around you. You can see them putting your coffee cup in the dishwasher or unloading your clothes from the dryer. You can imagine them living on the adrenaline of death, which does keep people going and going and going, talking and talking and talking, repeating the story over and over and over. Death is very hard on introverts, although even they rise to its occasion. You will hope that you have told your chief mourner(s) to relax, take time for themselves, breathe, sleep, walk, slow down. You will hope that they have listened. They probably have not. It is so likely that they are exhausted by the last days or weeks of caring for you that they won't even know how tired they are. If death comes suddenly, of course, that opens another kind of experience, one for which preparation is hardly useful. Sudden death is much harder than prepared death. In sudden death, we have way too many reminders of what yesterday was like. In prepared death or death after illness, we have the precious gift of time.

While you may not be able to imagine what is going on "down there," you can imagine that a lot is going on. You can imagine that they have begun to think silly thoughts, like what to do with your clothes or your snow globe collection. They may also be condemning you for being so disorganized that they don't have a good address book. They may also be angry with you for the way you went out. They may be displacing: why were you driving that road so late at night? You might have forgotten to say you loved them. Or tried to make a joke, even though nothing was really funny.

Of one thing you can be sure. When you die, the day after, those who love you or know you or had the coincidence of being your neighbor, whoever "they" are, they will be busy. They will be taking deep breaths. They will be thinking about their own mortality. They will be thinking about you. They will be talking about you. They will be remembering how and if you blessed them. You will have at least this day of fame.

THE MORNING AFTER SOMEONE YOU LOVES DIES

All that was said above will apply to the loss of someone you have loved. You will have the misplaced coffee cup, the laundry, the odd book that was half read, the unrecycled newspapers that turned out to be the last ones she read. You will have odd reminders of the deceased and they will be everywhere. The hospital bed may have to be removed. The hospice nurses may have to be told before they come for their night shift. And, on top of it, you will also be in charge. Maybe it will be your sister or daughter, son or brother, who will be in charge. In that case, your job is support. By support, I mean asking as few critical questions as possible. Somebody needs to be in charge. There is a way to be critical without being mean. Hopefully, you have learned that art by now. If not, be ready to learn it quickly. Why distract from the grief of a mother by having two siblings battle? Why distract from the grief of a husband by letting your offspring have at it?

No matter how important you think it is to call the undertaker right now or to tell Uncle Joe he can't come or to arrange the caterer or open the will, if the chief mourner wants to do something different, beware. You can negotiate a settlement and probably get some of your way. You can also "ruin" the experience of your beloved's death by going into an old fight about who is in charge or who has the most power or the least power or whatever battle is going on and has been going on. Predicting intimate rivalry is very important. If you make your goal to be the grown-up in the room, you won't have things your way. But you will have things a better way. If the decision about who is in charge at the end has not been made in the earlier preparations by the deceased, during which time it will have been very important to designate a chief mourner, then the first decision to be made is who is in charge. "We will defer to her daughter here. It is too much for her husband to manage." Or the opposite.

No matter what, name the fact that decisions are going to roll in like a tsunami and that someone needs to be in charge. Someone can be someones. Many people can operate like a team. Some families are even mature enough not to have fights at the

end. Spiritual preparation is trying to become one of those families or people before it is too late.

Some families will already know who the matriarch or patri-
arch is. Others will not. Why deal with anything but loss, grief,
and gratitude at the end? Allowing for a smooth process the day
after can be very important.

By the way, you have plenty of time. You have much more time
than you think you do. A lot of people will be rushing you, in
order to get relief from the pain of their own grief. They imagine
that if they "get things done" they will feel better. That is not true
but instead is one of those useful distractions that helps ease the
pain. When I say plenty of time, I mean that you can discipline
yourself for two hours a day to "make arrangements" and let the
rest of the time be as normal as possible. You can tell people that
you are just not capable of rushing. And you can also tell people
what to do when they ask that great question, *what can I do to
help?*

That question deserves serious attention. People will say it
with genuine mourning in their eyes. They will mean it. "Whatever I can do," they will say. You will likely have no idea what they
can do. But figuring out which of them is a good assistant or
general manager or project manager or manager of a difficult
person is a very good idea. Again, preplanning can help you a lot
here. Who is going to drive you nuts at the end? Who can handle
him or her? When neighbor *x* says that she wants to help, assign
her to relative *h*. "H really needs to talk. Could you call him?"
"Hi, H. This is neighbor *x*. We met back in the last decade at your
niece's graduation. Chief Mourner said she was worried about
you and had no idea how to connect, given all that she has to do.
Want to have coffee?" That may or may not work, for a million
reasons, but at least it shows you tried. Writing the obituary,
managing the reception, arranging the funeral site, locating the
address book, getting help cleaning up the house, receiving food,

buying food, picking up guests at the airport, taking the deceased's wardrobe to the Salvation Army—any and all of these things can be done by someone else. People really mean it when they say they want to "help." You will need help receiving help. Minimally, refuse to complain—or worry—about all you have to do if you hesitate to ask for help.

THE YEAR AFTER YOU DIE

You can imagine that those whom you have left behind are back in their real lives. You can imagine that they are "over" you after a year. Folk wisdom argues that a year is about right for an intimate—partner, spouse, child, mother. A year allows you to get through the first birthday, anniversary, Christmas, New Year's, and the like. The empty place in the circle has forced the circle to rearrange itself. It probably has by now. The glare of the empty space is no longer in everyone's face. Your chair at the table is occupied by someone else or has been removed or the table is in a different place. There may even be a new table.

Folk wisdom also says that we should not make decisions about real estate or automobiles or any large matters until about a year has passed. Your beloveds are about to make decisions. They may not need the big house or want it without you. They may never have liked it in the first place. They are probably getting ready to change and to transition into their new status of life. They may even have started to date. They are surely asking the questions about how soon is too soon. They probably still grieve you and love you but have healed enough to begin to have other relationships. They may even be having fun. I hope that my husband doesn't grieve me forever! Don't you? I hope that by the time I have been gone a year he has rearranged our table, our love life, and his future. I love him too much to want him bound to me in death. By the way, the old English wedding band is put on using these words: "Till death do us part." That means precisely that at death, we part. A new relationship becomes possible.

A healthy relationship knows how to change and make transitions. An unhealthy or overly dependent relationship doesn't know how to make changes or transitions. You will want to be especially attentive—all your life—to making strong relationships.

The day after you die—as I said earlier—your loved ones will be filled with thoughts and concerns and mixed feelings about you. The same will happen the day and year after your loved one is gone. Obviously it is important to clarify and understand that you are as different to them as they are to you.

You can't replace a daughter or a mother. But usually you can replace a partner, even if it is your best woman friend with whom you have always wanted to go on a cruise. And many people take on new "mothers" and "daughters" in lovely surrogate ways. There are plenty of people around who want to be loved. Be comforted by that fact for your loved ones when you are gone. And be that surrogate for someone else if and as you can.

If you are not feeling "over" it after one year, you probably want to get some help. Many people take five years to get through and over. Many people are ready to move on after three months. There is no right way to grieve. Instead, there are yardsticks. One year is a good yardstick. Plus, help doesn't mean you are sick or crazy. Instead it means you need help. Something is jammed. Life is short.

When I use the word "help," I mean reflecting on what is happening to you. Called "action-reflection," this is a deep process of self-watching. Like midrash regarding ancient texts, action-reflection is a form of personal participation in the facts of your life. You may watch yourself through therapy or pastoral counseling. You may watch yourself through meditation or reading. You may see yourself in others or in famous quotes.

Can you act and reflect on what John Quincy Adams said on his death bed? He said, "I am composed." Why wait until you are dead to be composed? William Blake said, "Death is moving into another room," imitating Gandhi, who said, "Death is a change of clothes." Why not watch yourself through the wisdom of others? Maybe you are just changing your clothes and moving into another room. You loved this outfit. You loved this room. Now you learn to love something else. You berth and birth yourself by entering into your own experience with your full acting and reflecting soul and self.

When a loved one dies it is a great rehearsal for when you die. You may be very surprised by what you experience—particularly if you give yourself permission to notice what you are experiencing. You may find that your responses are very unusual. There is always the possibility that you are having fun and don't want to tell anyone because they would judge you for it. So keep it to yourself, while understanding that love takes many forms and sometimes love fails to complete us. Not every loss is a "terrible" loss. The possibility that you might profit from loss can be very disturbing. What if the life insurance comes in and you enjoy having it? Be very careful to keep the "what I am supposed to be feeling" feelings at bay. Use a grief yardstick the same way you use a yardstick. Measure what you want to measure and let what you want to measure not measure you. If you have practiced using a tool like midrash or action-reflection, if you have learned the difference between blessing and cursing others, you will know what you are feeling and be able to communicate your feelings honestly. If you have lived too long in the land of should and obligation, or doing what others want you to feel or do, you will have a hard time with death.

Finally, even if you have never had a mystical experience or think of yourself as a mystic, be ready for a visitation. Many, many people swear they experienced the lost loved one in a mystical way, shortly after death. Many describe this leave taking as some kind of assurance from the dead that they are OK. I have no idea why this happens, but my most scientific of friends have reported it to me. Don't be surprised if something unusual happens. You are not alone.

MY LORD WHAT A MOURNING

We have always been heading for a conclusion. An end to the book. The end of the road. The fully eaten plate. The last paragraph of a great book. No matter how the end comes, there will be a sense of rightness to it. We will be surprised, of course, but a part of us will not be surprised at all. "It was meant to be," we will find ourselves saying. Death often has a touch of true. However it happens, you are changed. And those you love are changed. And "everything" is changed. No matter how highfalutin we get about the morning—or our final life meaning and how we have been part of it or failed to be a part of it—the morning after death will still involve mourning. It will likely be more terrible than wonderful.

There is no better time to do a life review than BEFORE YOU DIE. Trying to do so when sick and incapacitated just heightens the sadness. One of the best ways to do a life review is to think about what has happened to you and what you have made happen. Mourning turns into morning as we complete our life purpose or at least die while on the way to doing so. Mourning remains mourning the further off our life path we are. Grief is the larger the less we have stayed on our path. It is the smaller the more grateful we are for the time we had on our path.

A life review can be very simple and it can be ongoing, simply a regular habit of action-reflection that nudges you back on the trail of your life. Many of the most important things that happened to me aren't things that I made happen. I was headed toward that last paragraph all the way along. So are you. It has sometimes been good to be Donna Schaper, but not always.

Even famous people have trouble. Philip Seymour Hoffman died in early February 2014, up the street, across from one of the more exemplary families in our Sunday School. Hoffman was an exemplary actor. He also had a fault line deep within him. I'm betting our exemplary Sunday School family does too.

Hoffman's death plunged the users in the congregation—and our local NPR station—into near hysteria on the topic of drug use. "What if the insurance company discovers me with dirty urine?" Another, already using heavily and suicidal, said, "You know I don't really care about dying from this drug. What I care about is the intensity. I need to feel something. I need to feel recognized, noticed, useful. Nobody sees me. So I use. I don't care if I die. I am in it for the minutes." There are deaths that are self-caused. There are people who can't quit cigarettes or can't lose weight or can't stop stressing themselves with worry. By the time of death, we will want to know how many of our stressors were self-caused and how much responsibility we can bear for that fact. In a life review, there is no reason not to be brutally honest. The deception can kill us much more easily than the truth. Some things are our fault and some things are not. Remember what the son said to the father about how the turkey was cooked? "Dad, it's not your fault."

We will want to face our faults and also face what is not our faults by the end. Physical clutter is one thing, and spiritual clutter is another.

In my life review, I'd have to show the virtues and the vices. I was a nobody who became a somebody. By the grace of the Missouri Synod Lutheran Church and its preparation of pastors, I was saved, young, from a family bent out of shape by poverty. The Lutherans paid for my education and education brought me out of my family of origin into a larger and less pinched world. Then I became so self-important, so regularly, that I had to rag my riches. The more financially secure I became, the less grace I knew. There was a time when I could no longer imagine freedom from money and status. I became dead to freedom. Perhaps that was my first death and freedom rebound was a first resurrection. There have been plenty. Status was always my real enemy. I suffered from applause addiction, alternating with applause deficit syndrome. Both of these diseases paid well in money as well. The really big thing that happened to me was that a church gave me multiple gifts—of education, support, faith, hope—and that I tried to take credit for it. Through the process of understanding how gifted I was—meaning not talented but gifted—I came through my first death and resurrection. In the same way that we are born again and again, we also die again and again.

I already said we would sing the song "My Lord What a Morning. " And that we would scatter my ashes across the Hudson, expressing the upstate/downstate line that goes right down my middle. Will I be able to live in the city or the country alone at the end or still nurturing that split? Will I be complete at the time of my death? Only if I have one more turn-around congregation or organization? Or a grandchild from my daughter? One whom I get to know and covet and watch grow or graduate?

When I had breast cancer, my three kids were in high school. I made a bargain with God that I would see them graduate from college. God complied. I wonder if I can keep being such a good negotiator. And I wonder when I knock off the negotiations.

The second huge thing that happened to me was that I learned how to grow things. First from my grandfather in his strawberry/potato field in Kingston, upstate New York. But then from neighbors and books. Now I have a great garden. I am very interested in handing it off to the right people. True, I never could get the aggressive bamboo out of the backyard. I have gardening failures and successes. They matter to me as much as my failures and successes in love, parenting, pastoring.

Right now I am preparing to get out of the way of the next generation of clergy. It could be going better. I really don't want to retire, at least today. And I am at the age where I am receiving liturgical stoles from my retired friends. I already have a splendid wardrobe of liturgical stoles. There is one with a Velcro attachable mermaid. She comes on and she comes off. She is very useful in children's sermons. We now order boas in bulk at Judson for our ordinands, who increase in number and power. I love my work so much that I know I have to have a new job in learning how to get out of its way ongoing. I may have to give it up to keep it.

In the gifts from the church and the garden and in the mutual mentoring I have so enjoyed, I know the temptations of the gifted. Probably as you review your life, you also find that your strengths caress your weaknesses, which embraced then become strengths. That kind of action-reflection brings both the morning and the mourning on. It should.

I have already gone through my last golden retriever, after nearly a dozen over time. We even had puppies twice. I have already buried my best cat, after eighteen years of life with her. She is up the hill from me now at a place I overvisit. I am on my last job and hope I can last till I am seventy-five. I know I have taken my last road trip of three thousand miles. Too many aches and pains. I would love for this to be my last book, but I am convinced I have another one in there. That one will be called *Get Out of the Way*.

As you do a life review, it is great to stay on the path that is plowed in you, while simultaneously counting on your best-laid plans to fall through. Remember constant adaptive change? Probably by now you have had a good scare. Perhaps you, like me, are a cancer survivor. Or been hit by a drunk driver and came out unscathed. Or been hit by a deer and lived to tell the story. Very few of us get to be in early dotage without a few serious scrapes. As we travel from mourning to morning, it is important to remember those scrapes and what they taught us.

Breast cancer in my breast (not someone else's for a change) thirteen years ago brought me up short. It wasn't just my parishioners who were going to die or "pass on," in the euphemism. I will too. That experience made me less dimly aware of my mortality. I am not saying I am conscious of my mortality, only that I am less dimly aware of it than I used to be. An amazing grace attended me throughout the surgery, the recovery, the night sweats. It was the same experience I had when Pastor Witte showed up at our door and said, "Stop the fighting." This grace lives deep in my stomach. It was a grace that institutions had tutored. I felt it and shivered with it—and wasn't afraid.

Pastors see a lot of people die. Until that mammogram, it hadn't occurred to me that death was also in my future. When I talk about peeking around the corner to see what very few have ever seen before, or institutions getting out from under the influence of the old ways in order to imagine a future, I am also talking about the presumed private matter of how we see death. We peek around the corner. We move forward with faith, not knowing what is coming our way, but knowing that God comes along for the adventure.

The adventure is not ours alone. It is our habitat. It is our soil. It is our environment. It is the way we have or have not attended the systems that surround us. I internalized a lot of capitalism along the way. I was not always the master of my own material. When we think about our time, we are forced into some notion of God's time. Your God doesn't have to be mine or have a Christian metaphor. But your death will plummet you into questions about your origin and your destination, your habitat and your soil, the way you have gone with the flow or tried to swim against it. A day after you are gone, these questions will matter. A year after you are gone, these questions will matter. When all of us are gone, these questions will matter.

ASHES TO ASHES, STARDUST TO STARDUST

The Climate Change March on September 21, 2014, was intended to be the largest one in American history. By the time you read this book, you will know whether it succeeded or failed. It will do a little of both.

I have so many hopes for the march that I hope I won't sink it! I hope for a huge new investment in renewable energies and a cessation of investment in the dead ways. I hope for a resacralization of the desacralized, which includes the shale and the seeds, the water and the air, and you and me. I hope Americans will come to see our place in nature as much as how we see our place in history. And I also hope for a renewal of the way we die, right down to the words we use.

As you know, I've been saying "ashes to ashes, stardust to stardust" at funerals I officiate for the last year or so. I have been astonished at the response. It is pervasively positive. The language just slipped out of me after I watched Carl Sagan's show *Cosmos* light up the night sky. *Cosmos* reminds us that everybody who ever was is already up there overhead, blinking. When we die, we become a star. Why use the word "dust" when "stardust" binds our genome to a biological evolving eternity? Why frack when we can use sun or wind? Why stop when you can continue, even if in another form or way?

A renewable and renewing imagination need not start with the material, although God knows we have to do something about how gassy we have become. You can just start with that wonderful habit of action-reflection, of thinking about why you do what you do or why you are who you are. You can continue with preparing for your own death and turn that "job" into a joy. You can also start with spiritual practice and spiritual language. Spiritual practices are more like solar energy than anything else. They shine. They are an energy that creates more energy. Like solar, many people think they can't afford the long-term investment. Thus we stick to electricity or Lent or Sundays or candles. And of course, these spiritual surrogates are terribly, dangerously fragile. They are lightweights in a time when we need weight-bearing spiritual practices. Those who can't pray or renew or see will find somehow that they wish they had thanked or relaxed or seen. Those who think they die as dust will soon realize how much more fun it is to die as stardust. Plus, dying is one of the greenest activities of all. We recycle and compost our very selves.

Lots of people turn spiritual practices into confections. They are not confections. They are defections, when we disrupt the normal absurdities on behalf of the deeper absurdities. In those deeper absurdities, truth is lurking, with a patch on its eye. Or a star's twinkle, high above us.

CONCLUSION

Maybe my hopes for the future care of our planet are too small, not too big, especially if the energy we need is right here in prayer and in the stardust. For all I know, my hopes for my own death are too small as well. And at least, by finishing this book, I have encouraged you to be well prepared for death so that your hopes are not too small or too big but the right size, for you, instead.

FUNERAL AND MEMORIAL SERVICE PLANNING CHECKLIST

Name: _____

Date: _____

I wish to have *(check one or more)*:

   __ A service for the time of dying

   __ Visiting/calling hours for friends and family at the church

   __ Visiting/calling hours for friends and family at the funeral home

   __ Service at the church

   __ Service at the funeral home

   __ A funeral (body in the casket is presented)

   __ A memorial service (body is not present)

   __ Leave up to the family

Other:

_____

_____

_____

I wish to have *(check one)*:

    __ Burial *(before or after service)*
    __ Cremation *(before or after service)*
    __ Leave up to the family

I have made plans with _____
for

    __ A casket
    __ A vault
    __ A cremation urn
    __ Giving of body to research

Other instructions:

_____

_____

Approximate cost: _____

Location for burial or scattering of ashes:

_____

Service location *(check one or more)*:

    __ Church *(name, location)* _____
    __ Funeral home _____
    __ Other _____

Service to be conducted by *(if possible)*:

_____

_____

_____

_____

Person(s) to offer words of remembrance:

_____

_____

Music for the service (*hymns, solo, other*):

_____

_____

_____

_____

Scripture reading(s) for the service:

_____

_____

_____

_____

In lieu of flowers, I request that memorial gifts be made to:

_____

_____

_____

I have discussed my wishes for worship services at the time of death with (*check one or more*):

__ Family
__ Pastor
__ Other (*friend, executor*)

Names:

_____

_____

_____

Names and contact information of closest living relatives:

_____

_____

_____

_____

Will (*name and address of attorney for estate*):

_____

_____

_____

_____

Other (*health care proxy, power of attorney, etc.*):

_____

_____

_____

_____

Anything you would like to include in your obituary?

_____

_____

_____

_____

Please make your wishes known to your family and loved ones. We suggest keeping a copy of this checklist in your personal file or submitting a copy to your pastors. You may choose to do both.

GLOSSARY OF FUNERAL AND MEMORIAL SERVICE TERMS

casket: A fancy name for a coffin, though it does imply nicer fittings and trimmings. Preferred term for some because of the implication of the value of the thing it contains (think "casket of jewels").

coffin: The box in which a body is buried. Traditional versions include the simple pine box, as well as the hexagonal version (wide at the shoulders and narrow at the feet) you've seen in the movies. Connotes simplicity.

collation: A reception or gathering held after a funeral or memorial service; often put on by the church.

calling or visiting hours: Period(s) when the family of the deceased is available to be visited, usually in a funeral home, by those who wish to pay their respects—especially those who cannot attend the funeral or memorial service. Hours are usually published in the death notice and/or obituary.

death notice: A short statement, usually published very quickly in the newspapers of each area where the deceased had lived, of information including birth and death dates, and times and locations of services and calling hours.

eulogy: From the Greek for "good words." A speech that attempts to describe the deceased person and capture the truth of her or his life.

funeral: Worship service with the body of the deceased present. By extension, this usually happens within a few days of death. In some traditions, the funeral will follow a prescribed format.

funeral director, undertaker, mortician: A professional skilled in making and executing the plans, services, announcements, and equipment that many choose to make part of their arrangements.

graveside service: A short service that takes place immediately prior to the burial, or interment, of the body or ashes of the deceased. Often, but not always, by invitation to a smaller group than attends the funeral. Traditionally follows the funeral, but in the case of a memorial service, can and often does precede the service.

honorary pallbearer: In a service where the movement of the coffin is performed by professionals from a funeral home, honorary pallbearers serve as an escort or honor guard.

memorial service: A worship service at some indeterminate length of time (or distance) after a death has taken place, often after the body or ashes have been interred. Implies that the body of the deceased is not present. Often more flexible and creative than a traditional funeral.

obituary: A description, published in the local newspaper, of the biographical details of the deceased: loves, family, career, hobbies, education, or whatever else the family wishes to include. Longer that a death notice.

pallbearer: One of a team whose responsibility is to carry the coffin where needed during services and at the cemetery. Sometimes professionals; sometimes family and close friends. Formerly always male; now of either sex.

wake: Formerly described gatherings during the period between a death and funeral, for the purposes of watching over the body. Now tends to loosely describe any social gathering surrounding a death. Usually, but not always, takes place in the home of the deceased or a close relative.

WORDS AND MUSIC FOR FUNERALS AND MEMORIAL SERVICES

Never underestimate the need for music at a funeral service. Make it as good as it can be, no matter the expense if you can afford it. "I Did It My Way," by Frank Sinatra, is overused but often joins "Danny Boy" in releasing grief and bringing tears. Many people want a "three hanky" funeral. Let the music provide it. You can also sing some of the big hymns IF you think the people gathered can sing well enough to manage a hymn. For example, "For All the Saints" is a perfect hymn. And it is hard to sing.

> For all the saints who from their labors rest
> Who through the years their steadfast faith confessed.
> Your name, O Jesus, be forever blessed.
> Alleluia, alleluia!
> Still may your people faithful, true, and bold
> Live as the saints who nobly fought of old
> And win with them a glorious crown of gold.
> Alleluia, alleluia!

I Corinthians 15:52 is a very popular scripture at a service.

> In a flash, in the twinkling of an eye, at the last trumpet. For the trumpet will sound, the dead will be raised imperishable,

and we will be changed. For the perishable must clothe itself with the imperishable, and the mortal with immortality. When the perishable has been clothed with the imperishable, and the mortal with immortality, then the saying that is written will come true: "Death has been swallowed up in victory." "Where, O death is your victory? Where, O death is your sting?"

Or you might consider Jude 1:24, "Without fault and with great joy . . ."

The words of writers or poets may have special meaning for you.

This is my vow: To live content with small means, to seek elegance rather than luxury, and refinement rather than fashion, to be worthy not respectable, to be wealthy, not rich, to think quietly, talk gently, act frankly, to listen to stars and sages, babes and birds, and to do all bravely, to await occasion, hurry never . . . in a world, to let the spiritual, unbidden and unconscious, grow up through the common. Let this be my symphony.
(Adapted from the credo of William Ellery Channing)

I vow again to live alert to the rich deep murmur of the past. I vow to find the comfort in what has been. I vow to be unafraid of change, insatiable in intellectual curiosity, interested in big things, and happy in small ways.
(Adapted from Edith Wharton)

Now is the time to know that all you do is sacred. Why not consider a lasting truce with yourself and God? All your ideas of right and wrong were just a child's training wheels to be laid aside so you can finally live with veracity and love. Please tell me: why do you throw sticks at your heart inside? They only incite you to fear. Now is the time for the world to know that everything, thought and action alike, is sacred. Deeply compute the possibility that there is anything but grace.
(Hafiz, from "The Gift," fourteenth century)

Search the Book of Common Prayer for your favorite prayer. Mine is

Help us; we pray, in the midst of things we cannot under-stand,to believe and trust in the communion of saints, the for-giveness of sins, and the resurrection and the life everlasting. Amen.

(AN OPINIONATED) TEMPLATE FOR A FUNERAL OR MEMORIAL SERVICE

Prelude.

Opening Song. If you think the people can't sing well together or don't know hymns, hire a singer. You need music as it lifts the heart to grief better than any other medium. A lot of words inhibit grief. Music releases it. As a general rule, balance music and words. "Wordiness" is what you don't want. Well-chosen words are what you do want.

Welcome by Officiant. This can be a clergy person or a best friend. Somebody should preside and that person should know what they are doing, which is to hold the space.

Scriptures, Poetry, Prose of Meaning to the Person Who Has Died. Read by intimates. This is a moment of honor. Choose carefully and thoughtfully. Two to three selections is plenty; more than that number and people will get confused about what really matters to you.

Eulogies. Three is a good number. Use the chief mourner—the husband or wife or brother or sister or son or daughter. Use a work associate. Use a best friend. Again choose carefully and thoughtfully. If a group is planning the service, say a group of siblings, anticipate conflict. And then resolve it.

Open Microphones. Very lovely, especially if people know in advance there is going to be one. The moderator should hold this to about a minute per person. People won't abide by the rule but holding the space is what a good ritual does. Maximum of ten minutes here, otherwise crowd or congregation will get lost and nervous.

Closing Song.

Closing Prayers or Benediction. "Ashes to ashes, dust to dust (or newly 'stardust to stardust') we now commemorate your body to the earth from which it came."

Pointers. Discipline yourself to an hour for the whole service. Only go to an hour and a half service (maximum) if there are more than three hundred observers. This discipline will make the service beautiful, simple, and will allow for creativity. If you find you can't hold to a certain amount of time, you are probably refusing to make the kind of choices that will honor the deceased. Best of all, before we die, we should leave a folder saying what we like, who we want to speak, what we want to wear if laid out, what songs we like. Absent that, the chief mourners have to decide.

Consider issues like parking and weather and accessibility. Start the service no later than ten minutes after the time announced. People will come late. Many will also come early and on time. Honor them.

If you are a member of a congregation, usually all these services come without cost. Honorariums are still negotiated individually, especially with musicians.

Always print the full name of the deceased in the program with the dates of his or her life and death. Print music inside the bulletin so people don't have to fuss with the hymnal, if there is one.

Have a meal or a nosh or a collation afterward so people can stay with each other as long as possible. Have it as close to the service as possible. Hire a caterer so that intimates are not fussing with food instead of being present to people, or get your friends to hold, prepare, and clean up the food space.

Be considerate of accessibility in the hall. Many people who attend funerals are aged, for obvious reasons. Provide transportation for those you want there.

Have a guest book so people can sign and you can see who came.

Make arrangements for flowers to go home with the grievers. Make them in advance of the service, who will take what.

A funeral usually means the body is present in a casket. A memorial usually means that it is not and that an urn containing the ashes is present instead. The disposition of the ashes may happen directly after the service or at a later appointed time. More and more, people spread the ashes in different places that are important to the deceased or the family. If there is a casket, normally the interment happens immediately after the service and only the closest people go to the cemetery. When there is an actual in-ground burial, it is very important to know who will be the last person to leave.

BUDGET FOR A FUNERAL OR MEMORIAL SERVICE

If you belong to a spiritual home, there is usually no cost for a congregant. The congregant gets all the services free and also usually makes a special contribution.

Officiant: $200–$500, depending on what the person does. If they also do grief counseling, it should be the higher number.

Hall or sanctuary: $200–$500, depending on the size of the crowd you expect.

Custodian: $200.

Musician(s): $200 each, at a minimum.

Security: $200.

Bulletin or service program: $100. Negotiate whether you are doing this yourself or asking the sacred space and its offices to do so.

INDEX